SUAD AMIRY is an architect, and Founder-Director of RIWAQ: the Centre for Architectural Conservation in Ramallah. After growing up between Amman, Damascus, Beirut and Cairo, she went on to study architecture at the American University of Beirut and the Universities of Michigan and Edinburgh.

Amiry has been living in Ramallah since 1981; she participated in the 1991–1993 Israeli-Palestinian Peace negotiations in Washington. She won Italy's prestigious Viareggio-Versilia Prize in 2004, and her first book, *Sharon and My Mother-in-Law* was long-listed for the Lettre Ulysses Award for Reportage. Her most recent publication is *Murad, Murad*.

BY THE SAME AUTHOR

Sharon and My Mother-in-Law (2005)
Murad, Murad (2009)

MENOPAUSAL PALESTINE

Women at the Edge

SUAD AMIRY

Menopausal Palestine was first published in India in 2010 by

Women Unlimited
(an associate of Kali for Women)
K-36, Hauz Khas Enclave, Ground Floor
New Delhi - 110016

Published by arrangement with Feltrinelli
for sale in South Asia only

ISBN: 81-88965-59-6

Cover design: Alpana Khare

Typeset at Tulika Print Communication Services
35A/1, Shahpur Jat, New Delhi-110049

For my menopausal women friends who *lived for Palestine,* but sadly she could not give them as much in return.

When my father died in December 15, 1978, I was very saddened but also troubled that he did not live long enough to return to his house in Jaffa, 1948 Palestine.

When my mother died in February 27, 2005, I was extremely saddened but also troubled that she did not live long enough to visit my home in Ramallah, 1967 Palestine.

When my beloved friend, Mamdouh Nofal, died in July 22, 2006, I was very saddened but also happy that he did not live long enough to see what would still become of Iraq, Lebanon, Palestine, Syria and other neighbouring countries.

SUAD AMIRY

Contents

Acknowledgements

I am deeply indebted to Riwaq and Salim, who were delighted to see me disappear for the summer of 2006 when most of the writing for this book was done, thanks to Marisa Savoia, on the splendid "Terrazza Paradiso" on the isle of Procida, Italy.

I am most thankful to my beloved friend, Maria Nadotti, for her help and support in getting *Menopausal Palestine* published by Women Unlimited, India. Maria, whose translations into Italian were superb, has also been instrumental in promoting all my works.

Special thanks to Alberto Rollo who took me by the hand and guided me through the different phases of the writing when I most needed encouragement. Giovanna Silvia, also from Feltrinelli, read and reread the manuscript and gave me extremely insightful comments. Thanks, dear Giovanna, for respecting my voice and style of writing.

Diala Khasawneh, Vera Nofal, Penny Johnson and my husband, Salim Tamari, all read parts, or all of the manuscript, and gave me very encouraging and valuable comments.

I am indebted to my English editor, Ritu Menon, who

worked hard not only to transform my Arabic-sounding English into proper English, but also for her passion and commitment to this book. I am delighted to have my book published in India, a country and a culture very close to my heart.

Big hugs for all my beloved women friends who have been interviewed for this book. They've been incredibly patient and unconditionally supportive. Some gave me the go-ahead even though they were feeling a bit uncomfortable with the way I 'twisted' their personal stories or their loved ones. I beg their pardon, particularly those whose lives were, for logistical reasons, not included in this book.

And, had it not been for the contentious but encouraging feedback from readers of my previous two books, *Sharon and My Mother-in-Law* and *Se Questa e' Vita,* I wouldn't have had the confidence to carry on writing.

Preface

Unlike my previous two books, *Sharon and My Mother-in-Law* and *Se Questa e' Vita* which were basically about myself (since mothers-in-law and husbands don't really count), this book is about others.

While the mounting pressures of Sharon's army and my mother-in-law forced me to write the first two books, it was my personal shock, utter disappointment and deep sadness at having a fundamentalist religious party win the 2006 elections in Palestine, that hard-pressed me to write this one.

Though neither a feminist nor a lesbian yet, I had contemplated writing about my women friends for quite a while, partly as an expression of who I am, and partly as a manifestation of what I wanted to be, but couldn't. Our combined lives, experiences and childhood memories spanned, time-wise, from World War II to the Hamas election. And space-wise, from Boston and Ohio in the US to Como and Villadossola in Italy, Ankara, Nicosia, Rommani, Cairo, Alexandria, Beirut, Damascus, Aleppo, Amman, Jerusalem, Nablus, Bethlehem and Ramallah, where we all now live. And events-wise, from Abdul Nasser and Arab nationalism to the 1967 war; from the PLO golden age in Lebanon to its 1982 expulsion; from the 1987 first Intifada to the euphoria of the 1993 Oslo Peace Accord; from the coming home of diaspora Palestinians to the forming of the Palestinian Authority; from Arafat's three-year siege to his death in November, 2004; and from Hamas' 'victory' to Israel's summer war of 2006 in Lebanon.

Some of the women are of the Sixties generation, which I unfortunately missed by only a few years: "Don't worry, Suad, as they say, if you remember the Sixties you weren't there," said my truly Sixties friend, Ann, when I expressed regret for not taking part, and hence not recalling much of that decade, as I was 'schoolholic', and Amman, where I grew up, was not exactly Paris. But regardless of age, we were all of the PLO generation (1964–2006). It was Palestine or its absence which formed the centrifugal force around which our separate individual lives revolved ... slowly interlinked at different times, in different places ... to ultimately intertwine and intermingle in Ramallah. But for most, it was the beautiful, fated Mediterranean city of Beirut (which is being bombarded once again, as I write these lines) that embraced us and bestowed on us our first encounters: first love, first sex, first degree, first revolution, first dream, first rebellion, first everlasting involvement, first military practice, first ... first ... Unlike Palestine, Beirut gave to a great extent, but sorrowfully never got as much in return.

One thing I do know for sure is that we shared a past and unfulfilled dreams and aspirations; the glorious past was certainly ours, but sadly the future of troubled Palestine and the increasingly fragmented Middle East, is neither mine nor theirs.

"It is not fair to have Hamas win the elections; we already have enough anxieties, uncertainties and apprehensions in our personal and public lives, we can't possibly take more." It was this astute observation of my intensely menopausal friend, Varda, that made me realise the obscure relationship between my troubled menopausal women friends and my no-longer-friendly Palestine or what I purposely chose to call Menopausal Palestine.

It was Varda who alerted me that my larger-than-life and under-the-skin reaction to it all may have to do with my own middle-age crisis. Four days after Hamas won the elections, Varda together with Ann, came to visit me at home on an impossible mission: to get me out of the house, out of my depression, but also out to cope with the new realities whereby Israel's separation wall confined us (chambered us) and Hamas blew at the last candle. I had spent five consecutive days hiding at home mourning Hamas' victory, or more accurately: mourning my/our personal, political and social defeat. I somehow took things to heart and hence was totally overtaken by a deep sense of anger, but also a deep sense of loss; I was mourning the loss of my personal way of life, the society I wanted to live in, the loss of a barely-existing hope for a free Palestine, the loss of touch with my diverse Arab and Mediterranean cultures, and most importantly what I, my mother, my father, my family, my friends, my generation and many others stood for: secularism and pluralism which is now being 'democratically' replaced by 'global religious fundamentalism' and 'local nationalism'.

It took me a month or two to come to terms (honestly, I never did) with the fact that Hamas' victory was only a materialisation of *our* failures. A strong sense of estrangement and alienation took hold of me. I no longer knew who I am (we are) and what I (we) represent.

All I know is that for now, neither the *place* nor the *time* is ours.

In order to get hold of who I am I decided to write a book about my women friends, the '*typical*' women of *my* generation.

"But you're not a *typical* Arab or Moslem woman."

"I am 'typical' of who I am: a woman of a certain time in a certain place from a certain class," is my agitated answer to a more and more frequently asked (or stated) question in the western world, where all stereotypes are politically-manufactured. All I know is that I have lived 52 of my 55 years between Amman, Damascus, Beirut, Cairo, half of which have been in occupied, dwindling Palestine.

I never understood what 'typical' really meant, but one thing I know: I am not 'typical' of their 'stereotyping'.

However, I must add that what distresses me most is that since the second birth of Christ: September Eleven, *we* (Palestinians, Arabs and Moslems) have so far successfully played our 'role' by living up to their stereotyping.

But I also realise that writing a book about 'us' is an indirect acknowledgement that we are no more: for 'documentation' in itself recognises the end of a reality: the end of a generation; the end of an era; and the end of being the norm. Things cease to exist the minute we become aware of the need to document them. This, added to my own alienation, deepened my sadness. Nevertheless I started writing this book.

Unlike the first two books where the stories were mine and pressing within me, and hence putting them on paper was simple and easy—my love for story-telling made them flow effortlessly—the process of writing this book was completely new and different. For faithfully writing other people's life-stories, particularly close friends', was challenging in addition to being laborious. While writing my first two books cost me the loss of a few friends and acquaintances, in this book I wanted to make sure I didn't lose them *all*.

My initial idea of writing *the* (and not *a*) social and political history of Palestine and the Middle East (an impressive and ambitious book with a grand public agenda) through the lives of my PLO women's generation, was completely swamped by *their* non-stop flow of intimate personal stories; the many six to seven hour interviews started but never ended. I was no more in control of their narrative flow. And how, and who in their right mind can stop a menopausal woman from telling *her own story: childhood* and *coming of age* was where *they* wanted to go, and that's where I irresistibly went. For them restating who they are was done through shedding collective political memories and re-visiting who they were as individuals. For decades now they have been immersed in the collective and have been so out of touch with who they really are as persons and individuals. One thing they didn't seem to want is to dwell on the collective struggle. Perhaps the wound is too deep to touch now.

I guess the book which *I* initially planned and intended to write will have to wait.

For the book to become truly *theirs*, I had to ultimately surrender. And that was not exactly easy for a stubborn and egocentric person like myself. However, it did not take long for them to totally enchant me and for me to just let go: they soon tenderly took me by the hand to their intriguing private worlds: captivated me, revealed to me their intricate relations, introduced me to their mums and dads in addition to the many other fascinating characters of their childhood and coming of age. More than at any other time in my life, I valued them all and loved their fairy-tales.

The four-decade journey in search of virtual Palestine brought them a long way from their loved ones and hometowns. They simply followed the Star of Bethlehem: their heartbeats and John Lennon's rhythms: "Imagine there is no country ... and no religion to ..." But watching the Palestinian flag being replaced by that of Hamas on television made them take in that at least one of John Lennon's prophecies was right: imagine there is no country ...

Having come to terms with the fact that the book was *truly theirs*, I was faced with yet another challenge: how would one deal with issues of *privacy* and *sexuality* in the small-town mentality of Ramallah (believed to be the centre of the world by all its residents) where they all live now, and in an Arab world where all single women (not men, of course) are virgins as no pre-marital sex ever takes place; a world of fantasy and denial: no homosexuals, no lesbians, no incest, no rape and no child-abuse. Or, put more accurately: how can one be unfaithful to the powerful norm of a subtle acceptance of the untold and the unspoken in Arab culture.

All possible writers' 'privacy tricks' were used: I changed names, I changed places, I changed times, I combined characters, I used fiction, and still I can assure you it will be

Ramallah's biggest puzzle to figure out who is who in this book. Having done all I could to protect them (but also protect myself) from unfriendly gossip in an increasingly socially and sexually closed society (and government, of course), having tried all, I was left with two options: either combine all love stories and sex scenes in one 'fictionalised' chapter, or assume there was no sex in the city. Lacking the right hormones, I opted for the second.

Having made the cowardly choice of writing a book with hardly any love or sex scenes, hence minimising its chances of publication, I made sure to include in it the most irresistible, seductive and *fashionable* three topics which a friend of my husband, Salim, once complained about:

"It is impossible to get research grants or get published *nowadays* unless one writes either about Islam, terrorism or women."

With a typical sneaky smile Salim replied: "I for sure stand a great chance as I have been truly *terrorised* by a *Moslem woman.*"

SUAD AMIRY

Part One

CRIME

Only in Palestine would a sexy woman like Yara insist that she was menopausal. Her hormonal level was so high, even *I* could sense it.

Perhaps forty years of traumatic, stressful and nerve-wracking Israeli occupation caused an early menopausal Palestine; it turned a whole nation depressed, unpredictable, often out of control, hysterical and sometimes even suicidal; how else could one explain a majority vote for Hamas!

"Suad . . . I'm really upset with you, how come I wasn't invited to dinner at Darna Restaurant the other night?" asked Yara

Totally surprised I replied: "Yara . . . You're not *even* thirty-five . . ."

"Thirty-one," she instantly corrects me

"*Thirty-one* and you want to be invited to a menopausal dinner? Is it really that bad? Or do I conclude that there is no more sex in your life!" I looked her directly in the eye.

"No-o-o . . . I mean ye-e-es . . . I mean no-o-o . . ." Being single in Palestine where *presumably* no premarital sex takes place, Yara was a bit perplexed "Well, anyway, how come Rana was invited? She's not menopausal yet either … and I can assure you, she is *veeery* active …"

I didn't know what to make of Yara's remarks about her friend and work colleague. Not wanting her to dwell too much on Rana's sex life, or for that matter on mine or other menopausal women's no-sex life, I quickly interrupted her:

"The other night Rana said she was thirty-eight."

"Big liar, she's at least forty-*two* … if not forty-three." Both words, *liar* and *two* were over-emphasised.

"Se-e-e … she is at least forty-two … Anyway, Yara, it wasn't my decision to include her; it was CRIME's."

CRIME stood for: Committee of Ramallah Independent Menopausal Enterprise.

Not knowing what it stood for, Yara continued with her rivalry: "Yes, I totally agree, it's absolutely a crime to include Rana in anything. Ask me, I know better." Not wanting to get entangled one more time in their never-ending tribulations, I stopped there.

It was not accidental that the letter W, short for women, didn't appear in our acronym, CRIME, as we strongly believe that men are as *men-opausal (or women-opausal)*. But as is often the case, men are in constant denial: "Why do you need a menopausal group, is it really *that* bad?" "Why do women want to be *alone* without their men?" "Why don't you take me with you to one of *those* menopausal dinners?" "I am dying to know what it is you talk about in *your* dinners." "*Please* don't talk about our sex life to your friends." "Don't worry, darling, there isn't much to report," and so it went, with our husbands' disagreeable comments which often became a source of entertainment at our menopausal dinners.

I still recall the great fun we all had once responding to a note sent to us by Akram, Ola's husband. In it he offered his "services to *all* of you sexually deprived menopausal women". After spending quite a bit of time calming down the outraged Aida:—"This letter is utterly unacceptable, it is insulting and absolutely sexist … Don't understand why men think with their …"—we agreed her reaction was a bit exaggerated and uncalled for. Some of us ultimately had to take, if not Akram's side, at least Ola's who had naively brought his note to us. My overwhelming love and my strong sense of protection towards Ola, but also my irritation with Aida's holier-than-thou reaction made me intervene: "Calm down, Aida … enough … after all, there is something called a joke in life, even if it is a bad one, we can always get back at him." In no time Aida joined in in our written response mostly by reciting popular proverbs:

"Arab oil for Arabs," started Ola.

"Thy neighbour before thy family" (*Il-jar Qablil dar*), added her neighbour Flora.

"Save your white penny for your dark day … soon" (*Khabbi qershak il abiyad la youmak il aswad*).

"We won't believe until we see." (*Ma minsadeq hatta nshouf*)

And so it went.

Boy, was that fun.

Poor Akram, if he only knew how intimate and intimidating menopausal women can be.

For a while, we contemplated calling ourselves PMW (Palestinian Menopausal Women), but we were a bit hesitant, didn't want to be sued by BMW as most Palestinians pronounce Ps as Bs. Though ideologically and historically international *(umamoun)*, being anti-globalisation, the eight-member core group also declined to call itself G8. However, when Eve Ensler, author of *Vagina Monologues*, together with Jane Fonda visited us in Ramallah in 2003, a few younger CRIME members got excited and suggested we call ourselves the 8-G-Point. But the more realistic members thought that the No G-Point was certainly much more appropriate, and older members said there was No-Point changing our name.

CRIME Members

Oops . . . I've only now realised that not even *one* CRIME member is a truly 'blue-blooded' Palestinian! Our initial eight-member group, included:

One semi 'blue-blooded' Palestinian: Reem, with a half-French mother.

Two 'purple-blooded' Palestinians: Aida with a Jordanian mother, and myself with a Syrian mother.

Two 'pure' Arabs: Egyptian Ola and Moroccan Jamileh.

One 'pink-blooded' Arab 'minority': Flora, an Assyrian from Damascus.

Two 'foreigners': Varda, a Greek Armenian; and Ann, an American.

And, finally, one bloody Israeli: Ruth Blanc, as no international crime is possible without an Israeli. Since, for Israel, the three-and-a-half million Palestinian-Arabs do not really count, though she was part of the initial group, I purposely decided not to count Ruth, respecting reciprocity.

Being truly a Partisan, a veteran and a life-time supporter

of Palestine, the Italian European Parliamentarian, Luisa Morgantini, has been given honorary membership and honorary mention (hence her story has been included in this book). It was Ruth who demanded that Morgantini be given at least a three-life-sentence CRIME membership for being "biased" (short of saying "anti-Semitic") and blindly supporting the Palestinians.

Reem's obsession with searching for someone to fetch her a surplus of homeopathic hormonal substitutes from Rome, results in her having anxiety which by far surpasses that caused by her menopause. Her melancholic and sleepless face reflected her exhausting work as a press attaché in the late Arafat's office. Meeting journalists at the crack of dawn was the norm for the President. Reem, like others who worked closely with Arafat, has no explanation as to why he worked through the long hours of the night. Some say he, like old people, believed death arrives mostly at night. Others say he wanted to add a mysterious aura to his revolutionary reputation. But perhaps it was best expressed by a Russian diplomat in Beirut in the Seventies who was often awakened by PLO officials in the middle of the night: "Why is the PLO like a prostitute who works at night and sleeps during the day?"

With Aida, the chain-smoking health doctor, there is no nonsense: "Of course there *is* menopause: you simply go through it. Drive everyone around you crazy, and in two or three years you come out of it, often without a husband, but sound and fat."

Hormonal feminist Ola, on the other hand, swears that she, like her *Teita* (grandma), would continue to have her periods and all that follows . . . until she is at least eighty. If energy level is an indication of age, at fifty-five activist Ola has more of it than most of her university students.

Meanwhile, Jamileh's menstrual cycles were substituted by depression cycles. She had paid dearly by spending all her youthful years with the PLO: from Paris to Beirut to Riyadh, with the PLO to Tunis, and finally 'home' to Ramallah. Her depression cycles had always been in total synchrony with those of the PLO; hence Hamas' victory in 2006 knocked her out completely as it did the PLO.

Level-headed, self-controlled Flora insists that menopause is of our own making: "What menopause?" she argues. This fits well with her *anti-all* attitude: she is anti-conventions, anti-traditions, anti-religion, anti-nationalism, and most of all anti-minorities. A self-hating Assyrian, she substituted her minority mother-tongue with meticulous Arabic. Hence, she is an internationally recognised simultaneous translator from, and into, Arabic.

Varda, a kindergarten teacher, had been the main reason behind CRIME. She's had manifested menopausal symptoms: anxious, habitually suspicious, more often upset, never patient, increasingly jealous, and lately, hypochondriac and, God, is she . . . obs . . . ses . . . sive. Hers and her family's numerous migrations around the Mediterranean reflect the history and character of the Ottoman Empire. Being Armenian-Greek-Cypriot of Turkish origin, married to a Palestinian whom she met in Beirut, sheds *a bit* of light on her complex character. Being hilarious and cynical made some CRIME members refer to her as *hashasheh* (funny): "Only now I understand why the mother-daughter-in law relationship is stressful; she (Maha, her daughter-in-law) arrived at the worst possible time in my life, a time when I could hardly bear myself or put up with my own husband. All of a sudden I have to be sweet—which is totally against my nature—and turn the estrangement with her and her family into intimacy. Of course, it was not going to work."

Ann is a writer who spent her early life living in American air force camps, and the rest of it writing about Palestinian refugee camps. Unlike other CRIME members, Ann's menopause accentuated her pleasant character.

Being thirty years post-menopausal, Ruth, like most Israelis, has totally forgotten what she made people around her go through. However, once at Qalandia check-point, she regains her menopausal virtues as well as her Jewish argumentative skills and her Israeli aggression, by screaming back at the Israeli soldiers who scold her for having *illegally* sneaked into barbarously dangerous Arab Ramallah, let alone menopausal Ramallah. If the Israeli soldiers only knew the combined history of Ruth's CRIME friends, she would be the first Israeli Jew to get at least ten life sentences for being in touch with, let alone befriending, us.

Considering the English stutter that American Ruth has and her post-menopausal memory, it will probably take the Israeli Mossad, together with home security Shin Beit, thousands of hours to interrogate her so as to figure out whom, how and where CRIME members met one another in the long and non-kosher journeys of their web-like lives, which had a strong historical connection with highly suspect 1970s and '80s Beirut.

It was from Beirut's universities that Aida, Flora, Varda and I graduated. It was also in the Palestinian refugee camps of Beirut and around it, specifically PLO controlled areas which were referred to as 'Fatah Land' that Flora, Reem, Jamileh, Ola, Aida, Ann, Luisa Morgantini and I got hooked to, and ultimately became, Palestine addicts.

It was from Beirut that many of our friends left in the Seventies on difficult missions and never made it back. It was in Beirut that many PLO officials were assassinated.

It was to Beirut that Reem chose to go when the Israeli Shin Beit deported her from her house in Bethlehem in September 1978.

It was also from 1982 Beirut and its port where the ships carrying Flora's, Jamileh's and Reem's husbands, friends, life-time comrades, Palestinian fighters, together with their Chairman, Arafat, and other PLO leaders, sailed away. Like the rest of the other remaining fearful Palestinians civilians, the three of them stood there wiping their tears in the midst of a sea of friendly Lebanese who came to say farewell to Palestinian arms. Soon after, each escaped to their homes in Beirut and aimlessly went in one direction or another, finally reuniting in Tunis. It was not long after that the Israeli fighter planes, like fate, followed them once more, thousands of miles away, to their offices in Hammam il Shate in Tunis and killed a few more of their prominent leaders and friends.

It was in the many international women's conferences around the world's capitals that the 'insiders', Aida, Ola, Ann, Varda and I, met with the banned PLO 'outsiders': Flora, Jamileh and Reem.

It was during the Israeli-Palestinian Peace Talks in Washington, whose route passed through Tunis where the banned PLO was, that the relations between Ann, me (members of the negotiations team) and the three banned 'outsiders' (working with Abu Mazen and Arafat) strengthened. It was not until 1993 when Arafat and Rabin met on the White House lawns to sign the Oslo Peace Accord that Palestine became, at long last, their final destination. It was in Ramallah that the 'outsiders' now referred to as diaspora 'returnees', Flora, Jamileh and Reem, reunited with the other members of their future CRIME: Aida, Ola, Varda, Ann and myself. We had, meanwhile, made it back to Ramallah, Palestine for quite some time, long enough to be called 'locals'.

1

Ola

Alexandria, Summer 1964

It was Teita's love for life and for me that shaped the early years of my life.

   It was my mum's lack of character, the 1967 War, and my love for Jamal Abdul Nasser that shaped my youth.

   And it was my love for Palestine that doomed the rest of it.

"Olaaaaah...!" came the loud and commanding yell from behind.

   Recognising the voice I was terrified. I looked back—there was my father across the road.

   I almost fainted.

   He was standing right outside the barber's shop; half his face was shaved while the other half was still white. The barber's red towel, hanging round his neck, accentuated his angry red eyes.

   Like salt, we all dissolved in no time—I and my girlfriend Nadia in one direction, the two boys accompanying us in another.

Breathless I arrived at our summer house in Alexandria. I ran and instantly confided in my older sister, Amal. She was fifteen, I was thirteen.

"And who were these boys?" she inquired inquisitively.

"We met them on the Cleopatra Beach two days ago and this afternoon we went for a stroll along the promenade."

"Were you holding hands?"

"No-o-o," I denied vehemently.

Not totally convinced she said: "Right. To bed then, before Dad arrives."

This, of course, was not the first time I took refuge in bed to escape Dad's punishment. Lying there anxiously waiting for him to arrive, I was thinking how much I miss Teita with whom I lived till a few months ago. I recalled how some years ago, she stood up for me when Dad caught me in the street playing with fire with the neighbours' kids. The minute I spotted him from afar, I ran up the two flights of stairs which took me to *our* house—Teita's. Breathless, she instructed me to take refuge in bed. So, terrified, I held the red-hot coin in my hand and stuck it in my pocket. With my head under the yellow blanket, I was crying partly out of pain and partly out of fear.

My childhood episodes with Teita always ended with her taking my side, whereas my adolescence episodes often ended with a yell or smack from Dad. Unlike Teita, my eldest sisters were not in a position to intercede. My mum had no intentions; she didn't have what it took to mediate.

This time I was lying in bed crying partly from fear, but mostly out of longing for my thirteen-year life in Cairo with my beloved Teita. Until recently, she was my everything; she was my mother, my companion, my friend, my family and most of all, Teita was my spoiler.

Big time.

I was grieving being a complete stranger among five sisters whom I didn't love or trust, and four brothers whom I hardly knew or cared for. But most of all, I was mourning the loss of Teita as *my* mum. As far as I was concerned all mums should be like Teita— kind, generous, happy, strong and beautiful. But my new mum was nothing like that.

Teita was everything and Mum was nothing.
Teita was my mum, Mum was not.

I was three months old when Teita adopted me. My mother fell ill right after she gave birth, so couldn't breastfeed me. She didn't seem to mind having her mother adopt one of her four little children who, with time, became ten.

Teita was my queen and I was her *only* princess.

Like a little princess I lived with Teita Mariam and Grandpa Hilmi in al-'Agouzah, in the huge apartment located on the second floor of the three-storey building owned by my rich and beautiful grandma.

Yes, Teita was beautiful; she was tall, slim, with big green eyes and light brown curly hair.

Teita was elegant; she had many nice dresses and outfits, she had many colourful high heel shoes which I often wore around the house. She wore a little make-up, but lots of kohl.

Teita had lots of jewellery, mostly in gold. Like her I loved going to the glittering *suk-id-dahab* (the gold market) which was full of gold. I loved spending hours between the gold vetrines of the bustling alleys of Khan-il-Khalil. "Hold on to me, don't get lost," she would say as she walked quickly between the shops. I would be swinging left and right as I held tightly to her wide plissé skirt.

She bought herself gold rings, gold necklaces and gold bracelets. She also bought me gold earrings.

There was one gold necklace which I truly loved. "When I die you can take this one, sweetie," she often said as I sat on her lap playing with the many star-like decorations hanging around her neck. "And when are you going to die, Teita?" I would ask eagerly. She would burst out laughing and say: "Not in the near future, sweetie," and wrap the necklace around my neck. I would wear it proudly for a short while before she hid it in her safe.

Teita was also very rich; she had lots of money: she gave me some every day before I went to school, and she gave me lots on the big and small Eid. Teita gave money not only to neighbours and their kids, but also to many of her friends. She gave money to all *except* Grandpa Hilmi. I often heard her say, "You married me for my money, hence you get none." Teita loved everyone but Grandpa.

All who loved Teita, and they were many, also loved me. Her son, uncle Sami and his wife, Tante Amira, lived in the apartment above us. They had no children and I was their beloved one. Nana 'Alia, who lived in a small room on the roof, baked Teita and me hot bread every day; big loaves for Teita and small ones for me.

Tante Lamia and Uncle Mohammad, who always screamed at one another, lived on the ground floor. Uncle Mohammad habitually bought Teita meat, milk, fruits and everything else. Tante Lamia, who brought Teita all the neighbours' gossip, brought me lots of chocolates and ice cream. My friends, the neighbours kids: Hind, Muna, Naser and Hani, frequently came by to take me to play with them. "Stay in the garden, don't go out in the street," Teita always said as we hurried down the stairs. Teita also instructed me to run home the minute I spotted my Dad who came to see me frequently. Dad did not like me to play in the streets. He never allowed my sisters to do so. Pretending not to see me running away from him, he would often say: "Only the gypsies and poor children play in the streets." He would kiss Grandma's hand and call out to me:

"Sweetie, come and see what I've got for you."

It was only a minute or two later, after I came running to sit on his lap and grab all the goodies he had brought me, that I heard him say: "Isn't it time for you to come and live with us, sweetie?"

Both Teita and I would instantly and instinctively scream, "N-O-O-O!"

But that did not stop Dad from expressing his desire every now and then.

"You have nine, and I only have one," I often heard Teita reply angrily.

It was my infatuation with Teita and my resentment, and perhaps anger, at my mother that made me resist going to my parents' house, which was a ten to fifteen minute walk away from mine and Teita's.

It was not until the summer of 1963 that Teita and I fell into the trap. Dad's newly acquired TV succeeded in achieving what all the goodies, cinemas and even Ismael Yasin's hilarious theatre and Umm Khulthum's concerts failed to do.

Teita's love for TV made her take me to Dad's house more frequently than ever. I always sat, if not in her lap, very close, often clutching onto her. The minute I yawned Daddy would suggest I sleep there. Horrified, I would vow with Teita to buy our *own* TV.

"I can't stand being or even having a meal with him, for God's sake, do you want me to spend whole evenings around him!" with reference to Grandpa Hilmi. It was not until then that I realised why Teita always took me out to restaurants. She did that all the time, except when Uncle Kebab arrived unannounced. This was not his name, but that's what I liked to call him. Every time Uncle came, and he came quite frequently, especially when Grandpa was not around, Teita would spend hours making him kebabs. That was all he seemed to want, or that was all that Teita knew how to cook. Like his name, Uncle Kebab looked funny; extremely tall and extremely thin with very little hair in the front and even less hair in the back. I don't know why he pulled the ones in the back to the front and the ones in the front to the back. Everything about him made me giggle. And *that*, Teita did not quite like.

I woke up one night and Teita was gone. I roamed around my parents' house crying and asking for her. "Stop it, you're no more a kid and Teita has gone to her house," my Dad screamed at me and my mother repeated after him. I was in total shock. And I was in total fright; the moment I had always dreaded had finally arrived. Though the morning light was still faint, I opened the door and ran to Teita's arms and tears.

17

Not wanting to make a scene, Dad let it be once or twice, then his thirteen year old daughter had to submit.

Teita had an older person's grudge, and Dad had an Arab man's determination.

I spent my adolescent years taking revenge for the loss of my Teita's unconditional love by going against my father's will.

Dad may have succeeded in seeing me holding hands on Alexandria's open promenade this time, but I swear he will never be able to catch me kissing and hugging in the darkness of the stairway leading to his kingdom—our apartment in Cairo.

2
Aida

Ramallah, Summer 1958

Both sisters, Ruba and Lama, were in fits of laughter as they lent a hand to each other to rip scraps out of their school notebooks and stick *yet* one more sheet of paper to the expanding patchwork they were forming.

Tense smile on my face, I was uncomfortably looking at my sisters, a few years older, who kept giggling and repeating: "No ... not yet ... not big enough," and went right back to more patchwork. They were forming one *huge* piece of paper which would ultimately accommodate my BIG ass.

This, of course, was *not* the first time they hurt me by devising games around my ass. "Yes ... yes ... you can make it up the almond tree, but only if we manage to squeeze your big ass between the two branches ... Samir ... Samir!" they would yell at my eldest brother: "Could you give us a hand, ple-e-e-e-ase." Being a helpful kind of boy he would instantly leave his friends—who often came to play with him in our big garden or on the terrace in front of the house—and come rushing down the terrace stairs, two steps at a time, with his friends trailing right behind him. All together they would count:

"O-waane … Twoooo … Threee … and hoppa-lishaaa," and I was hoisted up the branch. A second or two of balancing myself and I *finally* made it, like other children, up the almond tree.

Suffering from vertigo, light-headed, I would scream for help to climb down. "Aida, we can't do that right now. We need to pick up some more almonds for Mama and Teita," came the scolding, playful voice of Lama from the top of the tree. Knowing that Teita would secretly pass on most of her almond portion to me I would sit still for what then seemed like eternity. My sisters must have learned this trick from Mum, who would place me as a toddler on an armless dining chair while she ran around the house doing chores. Terrified of heights, I would sit still on the cliff-edge for hours on end.

But this time, unlike other times, I had positioned myself strategically. Both palms gripped the sides of the armchair, and with legs bent at the knees, my feet functioned like brakes. All in anticipation of my sisters' attack.

After a fierce skirmish, my brakes ultimately failed me. Screaming and giggling, I was dragged by my arms and, as was often the case, I surrendered. Sat still on the huge patched-up paper which they laid in the middle of the cold stone floor.

"Okay … Move this way … no, not so much to the right … a bit to the left … yes, yes … that's it … tuck in your skirt." Lama was giving me instructions while Ruba ran to get the crayons. Eager to get it over with, I looked over my shoulders and, as instructed, carefully slipped the ends of my bright orange skirt under my bottom. "Okay, Lama ... let's start. I draw from my side and you draw from yours."

Ruba was calling out drawing instructions as she handed Lama a pink crayon and kept a dark purple one for herself. I was beginning to worry about how my ass would look with my legs stretched out in front of me, when I heard Ruba complain:

"Oh, no, it's not going to work this way ... ummm."

I was happy, seeing them fail.

"Aidaaaa ... why don't you bend your knees and pull your two legs in towards you, that way we can complete the circle."

All of a sudden it was a circle not an ass so, delighted, I obeyed.

"Let's give it another try then."

"Why don't you draw first, then I'll continue from my side," Ruba suggested.

Lama started from the middle of my back, where all asses begin, moved to my left side, and as I giggled, carefully to the front. She stopped *right there*. Ruba, taking over, started from *right there* and went back to where all asses end.

Once the ass-mission was successfully accomplished all, including myself, were eager to have me stand up and carefully step out of my pink and purple ass.

To everybody's utter surprise, my ass looked more like a big colourful heart!

"Are you happy now?" I asked revengefully, as they were both rolling about in laughter, looking at the drawing which they then took around asking everyone to guess what it was.

Both Mum and Samir took my side, the former out of sympathy.

"I agree, sweetie, it *is* more like your big heart. But in all cases this would be good a measuring stick for the diet which both you and Samir will have to start very soon," said my mother only half-jokingly.

"Right. This will also help us measure the space between tree branches before we push you up the almond tree," said Lama taking her Mum's comment as validation.

The heart-ass or the broken ass-heart was left hanging on the door of our bedroom for many days.

It was my ass in particular, my fat body (or obesity) in general, and the combination of my night-black hair and dark-brown complexion that shaped my self-esteem (or rather the lack of it) through my childhood and adolescent years.

It wasn't clear whether it was in addition to low self-esteem, or because of it, that I developed all sorts of fears and phobias; not only no going up the almond tree or any other tree in a garden filled with monkey-like children (brothers, sisters, cousins and friends), but no hikes or walks, no roof-tops, no edges of open terraces or balconies, no flights out of Qalandya Airport to Beirut, no elevators, and no escalators in Beirut's exciting shopping centres. And that wasn't all; my water phobia automatically deprived me from using the swimming pool in our country house, and hence the ability to impress the friends I *never* had—or the friends I never knew how to make.

Fat and dark, hence ugly, but as Mum often said; "*Clever with a musical ear.*"

Music haunted me while madness intrigued me. Or was it the other way around?

I didn't know which one excited me more—listening to my cousin Ramzi's music albums or *overhearing* stories of madness told by Uncle Mohammad and Uncle Anton. Dad's two friends would come in the evening, sit on the terrace with a drink in their hands, and talk about their patients' neuroses, conversions, hallucinations, etc. for hours on end. From my bedroom window which opened directly onto the terrace, I could hear it all. I was so receptive to these stories that I would get a real high. I often *became* the story. A momentary projection. I was trying hard to see the world from the madness point of view; to see why the world is mad.

Both music and madness made me cry.

"No, no, I don't want this. I want a record like Ramzi's," I was three or four when I wailed and threw away Lucy, my Christmas gift. Realising the big mistake she had made, Mum immediately picked up the doll from the floor, went out of the house and came back with the "*Love you, baby*" record. What with practising day and night, my voice was soon transmitted through Radio Jordan.

I was thrilled. Dad was proud.

"Thank God, you have a musical ear like me and are not tone deaf like your mother," Dad often said. This made me happy and sad at the same time. I loved it when Dad said nice things about me, but hated it if he also said bad things about Mum. Whenever this happened, she would give Dad a sad look, say nothing, but run out and cry.

Mum may have been musically deaf, but she was the one who bought all our records and books: "I want to compensate for my deprived childhood, but more important, I want to impress my arrogant in-laws," I often heard her say.

Whenever possible, Mum made sure to accompany my sisters and me to our piano lessons. Eager to get to Sister Annie's piano, I would always be ready half an hour or so early. I would go out on the terrace, sit on the steps and wait for Mum to collect Ruba and Lama who would somehow disappear just a few minutes before every piano lesson.

"Girls from *good* and *respectable* families (*Baant il 'Eial*) must go to *peinture* and piano lessons," I heard Mum tell Ruba as she literally dragged her by the hand all the way to school. Somehow, I could never tell whether Mum was serious or was making fun of Aunt Leila and Aunt Salma by imitating them. Coming from a modest background, Mum was always made to feel gauche around Dad's family.

"Yes, but not to a drunken eighty-year old teacher, and a sticky keyboard," Lama, like most of our schoolmates, hated Sister Annie.

Being the only piano teacher around, Mum pretended not to hear her.

Lama was right; Sister Annie drank red wine all day and had terrible pungent breath. However the minute she started singing and playing the piano, and the minute I started following her, I totally forgot about the smell. I had also got used to her sticky keys. She and I would play as long as it took for Mum to reappear.

It was a few months after Sister Annie's death, that Mum discovered I was musically illiterate. I could sing perfectly in tune, I could play the piano well, but I couldn't read a single musical note. Sister Annie and I were having a ball, until one day Mum said:

"Sorry, sweetie, no piano class this afternoon—Sister Annie has died."

I stood there stunned, while my sisters (and even Mum)

smirked as Lama repeated (or acted) what she had heard at school:

"Sister Annie went down the *cave* (French for cellar), climbed up the little wooden ladder, reached the top of the huge wine barrel and looked down into it. In her hand was a long wooden spoon. As Sister Annie scooped the wine from the very bottom of the barrel, she fell in. Head down. Legs banging against the sides of the barrel, while her head was totally immersed in wine. She drank and drank until her heart stopped. It took the nuns a few days before they found her in one of the many wine barrels down in the *cave*."

I burst out crying. They burst out laughing.

More than Christmas presents, I looked forward to Christmas carols.

While my sisters, brothers and cousins circulated around their gifts under the decorated Christmas tree in the living room, I circulated around the gramophone in the company of adults who gathered in the formal salon, used only a few times a year.

It was the recognition by Radio Jordan that made Dad and my aunts accept me in their adult performances.

Dad hated Christmas carols. He waited impatiently for the choir to end so that he, accompanied by Aunt Leila and Aunt Salma, could start their opera singing.

Almost everyone, especially the children, hated Dad's favourite opera singer, Enrico Caruso (or Errico as Dad insisted). They would roll about laughing the minute Dad started singing. Dad loved Caruso so much that he and his best friend, Uncle Khalil, made a special trip to Naples,

Caruso's birth-place. But Dad's greatest disappointment was when he discovered that Caruso had left Naples for London and New York half a century earlier. He was also saddened to learn that Caruso had sworn never to sing in his hometown. When Dad arrived in Naples and asked around, he discovered that Caruso had died thirty-four years earlier, in 1921, the same year Dad was born.

Dad also discovered what he already knew: he looked exactly like Errico Caruso; he was stocky, chubby, had a round face, thick eyebrows, black eyes, a big round nose, thin upper lip, was a bit bald. Except for Caruso's long moustache they looked like identical twins. Though a big disappointment, Dad came back with tens of Caruso's gramophone records.

Dad's Christmas costumes also resembled those of Caruso. Having seen the film, *The Great Caruso* at least five times, it helped him imitate Caruso's way of dressing.

Once Christmas rituals (carol singing, exchange of presents, tons of food and drink, children falling asleep and grown-ups totally drunk) ended, it was time for Caruso.

Swaying left and right, Dad would stand right next to the high table where Mum had placed the new gramophone. With as much concentration as he was capable of, Dad would take the record out of its sleeve and place it on the red velvet turntable. He would move the speed leverage to the 76 rpm mark, turn the black handle of the Manuela a few times, release the needle leverage, clean the needle with a cloth and place it carefully on the record. At that point Dad's eyes would glitter. He would square his shoulders and the minute he heard the music, he cleared his throat and in no time joined in His Master's Voice. Like the black dog with a white collar and green background on the gramophone, Dad also placed his mouth right inside the shining brass conical loudspeaker and started singing 'Recitar ... vesti la guibba' at the top of his voice.

Dad, Aunt Leila, Aunt Salma and I were the only audience left for the opera, and for the rest of the night.

Aunt Leila and Aunt Salma waited anxiously for Dad to finish his solo tenor so that they could join him in their favourite Verdi *Traviata: Un di felice, eterea ...,* and later, Bellini's *La Sonnanbula: Prendi, l'anel ti dono.*

Dad cried because he was drunk.

Aunt Leila cried because she missed her husband who had divorced her five years ago for a younger woman.

Aunt Salma cried for the dream man who never found her.

And I cried because music enchanted me and madness haunted me.

Despite all my fears and phobias, it gave me great joy to encounter one of the town's mad people (*majaneen*). Unlike most towns which had one or two idiots, Ramallah had four: Jalil, Laimouneh, Frida and Judge Nuri.

Early in the morning, Aunt Rima would open her bedroom window and stick her neck out in search of Jalil who would be down the street, waiting close to our house. At the top of her voice she would scream: "Jalil, Jalil, come up immediately! Take the money and go do the shopping for me." Before she could pull her head in and close the window, Jalil would be running up the terrace stairs. Aunt Rima would open the door, give him the big shopping bag, go through the shopping list with him, and hand him the money. He, on his part, would closely examine the money, close his palm firmly, and run down the

27

stairs. In half an hour or so Jalil would be back with a bursting shopping bag. But that did not prevent Aunt Rima from asking him about the *one* missing item which she had forgotten to ask for that morning. "Where is the milk, Jalil?" Jalil would gasp, slap himself on both cheeks, and go running back down the stairs again—and so it went. It often took two or three gasps and slaps on his cheeks before Aunt Rima decided she could wait till the next morning when it would start all over again.

Laimouneh was always seen roaming around the streets of Ramallah, holding a cucumber in her hand. She was either happily singing or enraged and screaming at people, particularly school kids, who would gather around her. Unlike most kids, I was not frightened of her. On the contrary I carried food for her which Mum gave me. I wanted to get closer to her but she stank real badly.

Frida, shunned by her family, stood on a small balcony on the first floor overlooking the alley next to our school. From her balcony she waved at passersby, making funny gestures and laughing hysterically. From a distance I would wave at her, she would wave back, then come to the edge of the balcony, hang down, swing her two long brown braids, at which point I would close my eyes in fear of her falling off the balustrade.

Mum and many others said that Judge Nuri, who lived close to Aunt Samia's house, heard noises, voices, weird things and strange screams. His domed house was in the middle of a huge untamed garden. It had close black shutters which concealed a daughter (or a son!) whom no one had ever laid eyes on. When madness came, Judge Nuri hid for days or weeks in the 'haunted' house, and when madness went Judge Nuri, very elegantly dressed, went to work in the town's court. Judge Nuri was by far Ramallah's best judge.

Mum used to say there were types and grades of madness; there is a silent madness and a screaming madness. A madness which is always present and a madness that comes and goes.

Now, some fifty years later, Ramallah's four idiots (not Foucault) turned out to be the main source of inspiration for my recent research entitled: 'The History of Madness in the Age of Unreason.'

However, this time the focus is not on the town's four fools, but on the objective context of a whole 'mad nation': Palestine.

3

Jamileh

Rommani, Winter 1954

My childhood oscillated between two different worlds: the simplicity of my father's peasant life: open, vast, spontaneous, and the complexity of my mother's character and the walled city that she came from: confined, restrictive, closed and regulated by oppressive etiquette.

My tiny knees were bent as my arched back rested against the huge solid dark green wall of the long and gloomy corridor. I was holding the hand of my baby sister, Lamia, tightly as she knelt against the same wall, next to me.

She was hardly two. I was almost five.

We were both shivering as we heard our mother's intermittent shrieking seeping through the door and window cracks. Her gigantic room was at the very far end of the corridor.

Every now and then Lamia and I would hear the wooden door-flap bang, and then see the swift leg movement of women who rushed in and out of her room. I gasped as I saw sheets and blankets smeared with blood stains being carried out.

Lamia and I were horror-struck.

It all started a little before the crack of dawn. We were awakened by Mum's excruciating screams. Father, in total panic, started running round the house switching on all the lights including those in our bedroom. Frightened and disoriented, we got out of bed and stepped out into the corridor. In no time voluptuous Salha and tiny Aisheh, our two housekeepers, descended the wooden stairs from their attic. Aisheh, though only ten, authoritatively commanded us to sit still as she hurriedly went to see to my mother's urgent needs. Salha, who was fully dressed somehow, accompanied Dad. Both went out rushing into the semi-dark streets of the ghost-like town of Rommani. It was not long before Salha came back with the chubby midwife, Sara, who rushed into Mum's bedroom.

Once again Daddy disappeared, this time in his car. He came back with Mum's four sisters. One by one, they were swallowed into Mum's bedroom.

Lululululuuuuuu ... lululululuuuuuuuuuu ... lulululuuuuuuuuuu ... came the loud and happy ululations of all the women in Mum's room. Until this day I can hear the multiplying effect of the ecstasy ululating against all the walls of the house, especially along the long corridor where my sister and I sat.

No one seemed to have noticed us.

"It is a bo-o-o-o-o-y! A baby b-o-o-oy! Yes-s-s, a gorgeous boy, as beautiful as his mother," I could hear Aunt Suad repeating joyfully.

"We must call him Karim (generous) because after *three* girls, God has *at last* been generous (*Allah Karim*)," said my other Aunt 'Alia

I wondered why *at last* and why *three*, when my eldest sister Salma, had died when she was seven months old, long before I was even born.

Until the birth of my brother Karim, I hadn't seen so much ecstasy in the family. I had never seen Dad jump up and down with joy. Not only was he in seventh heaven, he was *proud*.

Being the *first living* child in the family, I had (until then) been given lots of attention and love, particularly from Uncle Fuad. He often pampered me, carrying me on his shoulders as he went round doing his daily chores. But his tremendous love for me didn't prevent him from making two mistakes on my birth certificate: wrong name and wrong date of birth. Since Dad was not that keen to register the birth of *yet* another baby-girl, it was Uncle Fuad who volunteered. By the time Uncle got to the birth registry bureau, he had forgotten the exact date and was not sure of the name. Hence my life-time difficulty of having two birth dates and two names: Samia and Jamileh.

Even *he* overlooked me as he rushed in to see baby-boy Karim.

Lamia and I were starving as neither breakfast nor lunch were served that day.

By the time the *festive* dinner came round we had both collapsed, fast asleep.

It was a distressing occasion not only for Lamia and me, but also for the many sheep that were slaughtered for a night-long celebration.

I can't recall exactly, but it could have been my first encounter with the pain and anxiety of being ignored and unnoticed. Who knows, it could've also been *the day* when Lamia's unresolved, life-time conflict with Mum and Dad began!

All I remember is that many things started that day, and many others also ended that *very* day.

———————

"What else can you recall from your early childhood?" asked my psychoanalyst as I lay on her couch some forty years later, recalling the events and scenes of that day.

"Okay, your mother is reserved; hardly engaging, can neither express love nor affection … Mmm …" After a long pause Dr. Siham enquired: "Do you have *any* idea what your mother's childhood was like?"

I was taken by total surprise by my therapist's sudden shift. I was challenged by her question. For months she had focused on *me*, on *my* depression and *my* childhood. Why this shift now?

All my life I had suffered from Mum being *the centre of attention*. In reality this was perhaps *why* I sought therapy.

Having an early menopause, at the age of forty, was most likely the reason for my depression. But aren't mothers often the main reason for depression too, even if they aren't Jewish (I mean mothers)?

In my case, my mother's dashing beauty was the cause of it all: "Is she your mother? Wow! She's absolutely stunning! How come none of you are as beautiful?"

People would often tell Lamia and me this with a straight face. We both wondered if Mum would *ever* get old and ugly. Actually we looked forward to that day, but when *that day* finally arrived, people started saying: "Your mother must have been a beauty when she was young!" And so it went.

For a while, I just looked at Dr. Siham, then started thinking about my mother's childhood; in reality until this very moment, I hadn't realised that I knew absolutely nothing about her life, let alone her childhood.

Intimate relationships were not exactly Mum's strong point. She could never be intimate either with us, her children, or with Dad (at least not in front of us), or with the friends she hardly had, not even with her favourite sister, Suad.

In spite of the big fuss about the birth of my brother, Karim, and later my younger brother, Hasan, soon *all* of us were equal—Mum never gave any of us a hug, a squeeze or a cuddle. I fondly remember the embraces and cuddles of Salha, our housekeeper. The warm kitchen where she spent most of her time, added a powerful affection to her already warm and voluptuous body. She was our refuge for love.

My mother's obsession with her beauty, her slim and tall body, made it seem distant and cold. She lived in a world of her own, a world which was physically, emotionally and psychologically remote, at least from us children. "Get your room organised, do your homework, and read that book I brought you the other day," she would instruct each one of us before she put on her make-up and wore one of her many elegant evening dresses with jewellery that matched it perfectly. And off she would go with Dad for a movie or a dinner party in her beloved Rabat.

Mum's closed and convoluted character contrasted sharply with my father's simplicity, openness and love. She came from the alleys of the walled old city of Rabat while he came from the peasant world of Rommani. The openness of the large farm on which we lived as children, gave us the vast distances and the freedom we all sought.

Until I was twelve, we lived close to the northern town of Rommani. Our house was located in the middle of a huge ex-French farm which my father rented from the government. Next to the house were two large workshops: one for maintenance, the other for storage, in addition to the many stables. A kilometre or two away was the farm workers' little mud village. When not at school in Rommani, my sister and I (with Karim and tiny Hasan dragging behind) often played with the many sons and daughters of the farmers who helped my Dad raise sheep, milk cows, produce dairy products and provide meat for the butchers in Rommani. The farmers also helped Dad grow vast amounts of wheat. Of all the farm activities (in addition to donkey rides *and falls*), we looked forward most to the long festive evenings of the harvest season. In addition to all the farmers' children, tens of cousins arrived in the company of aunts, uncles and friends. I recall vividly the tunes and melodies of the many harvest songs and the delicious taste of the barbecued wheat with lamb. This was perhaps the one day in the year when peasant life demonstrated superiority over city haughtiness.

Harvest time was my favourite season until I was twelve. One day, unexpectedly, I found myself all alone at home with Dad and Mum. Mum had made up her mind to send "troublemaker" Lamia, but also Karim and little Hasan, to a

35

boarding school in Rabat, where her sisters and brothers lived.

Lamia was utterly outraged, Karim and Hasan (seven and six) were sulking, I was truly resentful, Dad was hesitant, but Mum was adamant: "What's wrong with that? All aristocratic families in Rabat send their children to boarding school," she would reply whenever one of us expressed dissatisfaction with her arbitrary decision.

"But we're neither aristocratic nor in Rabat. Poor Hasan, he's hardly six," objected Dad, *only* once, then kept quiet. Most of their disputes were about her hometown Rabat.

"I was hardly six months, not even six years, when *my* mother sent me off to her mother and sisters to look after me. I stayed with them till the day I got married," Mum replied bitterly. I was tempted to ask if she was taking it out on her children, but like Dad, I kept quiet.

"Lamia, if you don't gather your belongings immediately, I will have to send you off with no clothing," Mum was screaming at my sister who had locked herself in our bedroom in yet another attempt to have Mum change her mind about boarding school. While Mum was banging at Lamia's door hysterically, Aisheh and I were nervously helping Karim and Hasan get ready. I was praying hard that, this time, Lamia's stubbornness would triumph over Mum's. But I was wrong: soon I stood on the wide stairs in front of our farmhouse, in the company of Salha and Aisheh, waving goodbye to my beloved brothers. Perhaps my loud cries and tears were a gut reaction to what would turn out to be life-long troublesome and awkward family relations. I still recall little Hasan clinging to Mum, while Karim dragged weeping Lamia behind him.

The three were swallowed up by Dad's car which pulled away along the narrow and winding little farm road. Little did I realise then that with their disappearance, our beautiful and innocent shared childhood memories would cease forever, as would our shared lives and experiences.

It was almost dark when, with sinking heart, I walked home to Salha's warm kitchen. I stood there and asked hesitantly:

"Nanny ... How do your children feel, away from you?"

Totally stunned, she replied: "Habibti Jamileh, life often forces us to do things we don't like. I've got to earn a living so my children can have a decent life." With tears brimming in her eyes she stood up, came close and hugged me tight.

Being totally in love with Salha, I sort of forgave her.

It was Mum whom I never forgave.

Impatiently I waited for weekends as lonely weekdays never ended.

My heart would start beating the moment Dad's car reached the road sign which read "City Limits of Rabat", and I knew it would only be a matter of nine or ten minutes before I was reunited with my sister Lamia, Karim and my beloved Hassouneh (short or rather long for little Hasan). Uncle Fuad would make it a point to fetch them from boarding school before we arrived.

It was in Uncle Fuad's huge depots, rather than in his big villa and lush garden, that the four of us and Uncle Fuad's children would spend the two day weekend playing hide-and-seek, in addition to opening almost every little or big box of his varied merchandise.

From now on, it was summer, rather than harvest time, that I looked forward to. It was on the beautiful seashores near Rabat that we and all my aunts and uncles rented chalets for the summer months. Joining my sister, brothers, cousins and friends for a whole day of playing and swimming and late-evening strolls along the promenade, with many cafés and restaurants packed with Moroccans and blond tourists, became much more exhilarating.

Coming of Age

1963

I was thirteen, he was hardly eighteen.

Like the rest of us, I was totally mesmerised by the beating of the frog's tiny heart. That day Faris, a first year medical student, accompanied my cousin Sami to Uncle's Fuad's chalet on the beach. Faris, not exactly handsome, was rather funny. Trying to entertain and perhaps impress us, Faris had laid a frog on its back, pinned its four legs to a small cutting board, and with a sharp knife opened wide the skin around the frog's heart.

Despite my fright, I was impressed with Faris' surgical skills. While everyone screamed and jumped back I, trying to make an impression, gathered up my courage and stepped closer to the surgeon and his operating table.

Having heard our screams, Mum, Aunt Suad and Uncle Fuad stepped out of the chalet. As was often the case, Mum watched us from a distance, while Uncle joined in the youngsters' joy and excitement. I was so captivated by "Faris' Show", that I hardly noticed Uncle Fuad who stood next to me with an arm around my shoulders. It didn't take long for

Mum to realise that while everybody's hearts were beating for the frog, mine was beating for the surgeon.

"No need to act loose and indecent! You must behave respectfully around men," my mother's stern and uncalled for words took me by total surprise.

Leaving all the fun behind I ran to the kitchen, embraced Salha, and cried.

Salha was aware that Mum had been treating me bizarrely ever since I got my periods: "You can no longer stay overnight at your uncle's house. Make sure you're not alone in the same room with Sami or Sameh," referring to my two adorable male cousins.

"Beware of boys at school."

"There are *things* in life you'll learn once you grow up," she would repeat, sensing my perplexity and confusion.

What *things*?

How could Mum not be aware that all my 'sex education' came naturally as I had grown up on the farm, in close company with animals, farmers, little boys and girls? Could our *thing* be very different from that of Nura and 'Antar, our two lovely dogs? Doesn't Mum remember how the mewing of Paco, Lulu and their numerous cat friends kept us up almost the whole month of March? How different could our *thing* be from that of donkeys, horses and mules?

Why does Mother always pretend not to know? Or could this be because of her uptight city upbringing?

One of the more exciting aspects of going to the French Lycée in Rommani was passing by the Street of the Bordellos almost daily. Like Mum, we made sure not to mention its name. *There,* all kind of *things* must have happened. In the company of our curious classmates, we would cross the main road and watch the prostitutes on both sidewalks; some were French, others Moroccan. All waiting for a rich client. Our excitement and imagination went wild once the deal was sealed and both disappeared behind closed doors.

I vividly remember the strong feeling of emptiness which hit me when they suddenly vanished—they seemed to have dissolved one day in 1956 together with the French colonial regime. Their memory comes back every Independence Day. With the joy of independence came a sharp sense of sadness at losing many of my French schoolmates and teachers, especially my beloved Mademoiselle Claudine. Her house was a source of warmth and tenderness away from home. She often read and sang for me and sent me away with a French novel or two. For years to come, and in homage to Mademoiselle Claudine, I continued to read French poetry and listen to French songs and music.

That seemed to be the nature of all major political events in Morocco and the areas around; independence or wars automatically meant the loss of more personal friends, schoolmates, neighbours and acquaintances.

The Sixties and my coming of age seemed to be politically tormented.

As the French army withdrew, huge crowds came out on the streets celebrating independence. Egyptian President Nasser and many others came to celebrate with us. With schoolmates and friends, I joined in the street chanting and clapping: "Palestine ... ta, ta, ta ... Palestine, ta ta ta ... Palestine, ta ta ta ..."

"Dad, what is Palestine?" Our independent country is called Morocco and Nasser's country is called Egypt, so why are people chanting "Palestine"? I wondered.

"Dear Jamileh, Palestine is an Arab country which has been occupied by the Israelis. They kicked the Palestinians, who had been living there for thousands of years, out of their homes, took their land and settled there. As a result many Palestinians have become refugees."

What a terrible thing to do, I thought to myself.

How unkind.

Until Monday June 5, 1967, this remained my only piece of information about Palestine. That was the day I saw my father cry for the first time. "*We* have been defeated forever; *we* have lost *all* of Palestine; it will be impossible from now on to ever have peace in this part of the world. Oh, God! Palestine, we have lost you forever!" my father kept repeating as he wiped his tears, turning his face away from us.

Both Dad's *tears* and the use of the pronoun 'we' stayed with me.

The great loss of *all* of Palestine to the Israelis, in time, strained good relations between Jewish and Moslem neighbours in Rabat. Soon this was followed by the great loss of my Jewish friends, schoolmates, family doctor, dentist, seamstress and the owner of a wonderful jewellery shop in the old town of Rabat where my mother often went to buy her pretty jewellery.

By that time we had left Rommani and came to live in the old town. The Jewish Synagogue in the old town was located right behind our house. As a reaction to losing the 1967 war, crowds took control of the streets, thousands of demonstrators were chanting anti-Israel, anti-Arab government and most surprisingly, anti-Nasser slogans.

All of a sudden there was a big commotion in our neighbourhood. In the company of Uncle Fuad and Karim, I rushed down to the alleys where gangs of young men were shouting anti-Israel and anti-Jewish slogans. A few were running in the direction of the Synagogue, carrying gasoline containers. Many others rushed to protect the Synagogue, but also the Jewish family living by the Synagogue. Others were trying to protect the many other Jewish families and shops in the neighbourhood. Karim and I ran behind Uncle Fuad who went to protect our neighbours, also Karim's best friends. It was a while before the police came and took control of the situation. Material assets were saved that day, but sadly, centuries' long Jewish and Moslem friendships disappeared forever.

"Stop this madness, these innocent people have nothing to do with Israel, they are Moroccans, like us. Do you understand?" we heard Uncle Fuad scream at the demonstrators. Until that moment I had no idea of the relation between the 1967 war, Israel and Moroccan Jews!

I could only relate to what was happening in Morocco and many other Arab countries when I went to school in September of that same year, it was only then that I understood what it meant. Of the thirty-some students in my class alone, seven or eight had disappeared; they had left Morocco with their families; some for France, others for Israel.

In no time everything changed; all my friends, class- and schoolmates, neighbours, shops, and for that matter, all of Morocco, had become all-Moroccan and all-Moslem. How very sad! Only five years earlier many of my schoolmates had been French, Italian, Greek and Jewish. They had all disappeared.

Walking in the streets of Paris, where I went to study a year later, I often stared hard at people's faces hoping to come across Simon, my Jewish classmate, or Mademoiselle Claudine whose memory had been preserved in Edith Piaf's deep and sad voice.

Most of *all*, I was praying to somehow one day encounter voluptuous Sara, our Jewish midwife, who not only helped Mum give birth to my brother, Karim, but also gave me that reassuring first hug the minute she pulled me out into this difficult world—a very long eighteen years ago.

4

Flora

It was the heavy breathing close to my neck that made me suspect there was something fundamentally wrong with the black and white prints being shown to me by my mentally handicapped cousin.

He was thirty.

I was nine.

The delicacy and nuance of those skilfully illustrated nude figures in various positions have absolutely no relation to the crude porno images of today.

The difference intrigued me.

That afternoon my mother had sent me to her cousins' house which was only a three-minute run away from ours, the nearest in our isolated neighbourhood. Our neighbour-less building had Dad's clinic on the ground floor, our house on the first, and a roof garden on top. I often longed for a real *hara* (neighbourhood), where children played hide-and-seek in the alleys and spent time in each others' homes. Ours was

44

totally cut off from the populous neighbourhoods of Damascus and its bustling old town, which I came to know and value when I was much older.

Aunt Ermine's house was one of the two houses my mother felt was safe to send me, and later, my younger brother George, to. I resented it, because I would much rather have spent the time with Aunt Helga's four children who were closer to me in age, but her house was much farther.

A one-minute run up the stairs led me to Aunt Ermine's flat, a sharp knock at the knob of her metal door got her to open the door for me. With a cheerful hello from her, I walked towards the spacious but gloomy living room. Amidst the cramped furniture of their parent's house, I spotted my dentist uncle, Noel, and his mute and deaf brother, Bibi, who was the youngest of the three. I kissed them both on the cheek and quickly settled down on the comfortable couch next to the window from where a little light came in. I mechanically answered all the hows and whys concerning my Mum, Dad and toddler brother, George. Then promptly opened one of my many cherished books which I always held close to my chest.

I was totally absorbed in reading when Aunt Ermine disappeared into her little domain from where came the strong smell of afternoon coffee. As was often the case, the one hour siesta for all was followed by cups of coffee which gave my mother's two male cousins the energy to make it back to their clinic. In spite of his handicap, Bibi (never referred to as an uncle) was quite handy; he sat quietly on the counter behind the reclining dentist seat, preparing fillings and carving the caps.

With sideways glances, and as discreetly as my big eyes

would allow, I was looking at Uncle Noel's and Uncle Bibi's sign language. "Don't stare at him!" my mother would instruct me because I was totally captivated by their non-verbal communication. I was trying to guess what was it all about when I heard Aunt Ermine say, "Just leave your brother alone; he is obviously not in the mood for work this afternoon."

"Why didn't he tell me before? I could have asked Sami to pass by and help me with the caps."

"Well ... just try to do without him, or have them wait a day or two, it's only a tooth cap." Referring to his patients.

What intrigued me even more than their sign language was how my mother's three cousins argued constantly; perhaps that was one reason why neither of them had had the urge to marry.

Up until that moment, I knew nothing about the urge for sex.

Uncle Noel, not totally convinced, picked up his hat from the table and walked away, slamming the heavy door behind him. This gave me the needed excuse to overtly watch the scene; I could see Aunt Ermine's victorious expression and a naughty smile breaking over Bibi's lips.

Aunt Ermine went back to her kitchen, I opted for more reading. Though utterly bored, I often made use of the quietness of their house, particularly when each of them was occupied in their three different worlds; Aunt Ermine's kitchen and cellar, Uncle Noel's cavities, Bibi's day-dreaming. This gave me the peace of mind to be totally absorbed in a world of my own making, that of book fantasy. Reading breaks took me around their cluttered house, discovering interesting objects and possessions away from judgemental family eyes.

46

I was taking pleasure in the quietness of this world, thinking how wonderful life would have been around our house, *if only* we had a mute and deaf grandmother. Only mute, even better perhaps.

"Flora! How many times do I have to tell you, *not this* way, *sweetie.*" She would constantly instruct me in Assyrian, a language I understood perfectly, though I purposely resisted speaking it.

"*Leish laa, Teita?* (Why not, Granny?)" I would answer her back in Arabic.

"First of all, *as a girl*, it is high time you learnt how to serve coffee on a proper tray, and secondly, you should make *a bit* of an effort to speak your *own* language."

"I am speaking my *own* language, Teita. Having lived all your life in an Arab country, isn't it high time *you* spoke proper Arabic?"

It was the first time ever I had had the courage to confront my grandmother openly. Being calculating, I was taking advantage of her tense relation with my mother—I had overheard their heated argument the night before.

"Assyrian was the language of this land for thousands of years before it was downgraded by Arabs and Moslems. Get your history straight, *sweetie.*"

There she goes once again. I totally lost it: "Yes ... yes, Teita, by now I've learnt it *all* by heart: we are Assyrian and we are Protestants, and we are better educated and more cultured than non-Protestant Assyrians, and of course we are far superior to all Arabs and Moslems. Is there anything else I need to learn from you, *sweeetiiie?*"

Before she could get back at me I continued in Arabic: "Oh,

yes . . . *and as a girl* it is high time I learnt how to serve Arabic coffee on a proper tray, what else, Teita? How come you like Arabic coffee? How come after *thousands of years* the Assyrians have not been able to invent their own coffee?"

I was stressing every single word, as children often do, whenever outraged.

What got me most were her really condescending remarks about my non-Assyrian, non-Protestant friends, her not-so-subtle enquiries about my schoolmates' religion and her disapproval of my two closest friends, Maha and Mona, whose Arabic names I just adored. The combination of my grandma's unsettling voice and the *sweetie girl* thing really got to me.

From a distance I could hear my mother yell in English, a language we spoke at home for sheer functionality, not prestige: "That's *it* . . . enough . . . we're sick and tired of these repeated arguments. Why don't *you two* just stop that nonsense?"

I never knew what to make of my mother's compromising *you two* position when it came to arbitrating between me and her mother-in-law. If only my father were around he would have stood up for me. I was praying that his two-year internship in America soon came to an end for I was missing his authority, and his boy-girl equality.

With tears brimming in my eyes (which I made sure to hide) I ran to my room and locked the door for many hours. Once my anti-Grandma and my anti-Assyrian, anti-Protestant emotions settled down, I looked for my sixth-grade history book.

There was nothing of relevance in it.

To win a point, I settled for my Arabic language book.

And to win another point I swore to never again accompany Teita to Sunday Mass. And once Dad got back, I would go with him to the once-or-twice-a-year wedding ceremonies.

If only Dad were here tonight, he and I would have talked about world affairs, especially about history. Unlike Teita, he was proud of my knowledge.

My day-dreaming was interrupted by Aunt Ermine's enquiry asking if I was in the mood for patchwork. Hesitant to leave my book, I escorted her downstairs. Recalling my arguments with Grandma had made it difficult for me to follow the plot of the book. Patchwork on my aunt's never-ending quilt was sort of soothing. I was sitting next to her tracing the floral design while she cut colourful pieces of different fabrics. She then stitched them precisely on to her huge white quilt. For months it was neatly spread out on bedsheets occupying almost the whole of the cellar's patterned floor. After spending what felt like a long time in the cellar with her, I asked to go upstairs to finish the few pages left in today's book, and to check on the pre-sunset light outside, signalling that it was time for me to run back home.

Bibi was now sitting on a dark brown leather chair next to a crammed desk, totally engaged in flipping through the pages of his thick book. As I was settling back on my couch I saw him signal to me to come closer. Keen to learn his sign language, I ran up to him happily and stood right next to him. With a deep sigh and a big smile, he put his arm around my shoulders and gave me a big hug, then let go of me and went back to flipping through his book, pointing at its pages. Curious about everything, especially books, I happily looked at a few pages with him, but soon realised there was something fundamentally wrong about these charmingly drawn nude figures of men and women in different positions. Bibi reached out for another hug. I shrugged and said "NO" loudly. He put his finger on his rosy lips to keep me quiet. I kept quiet for the next two minutes, as long as it took me to get back home.

It must have been the heavy breathing that made my mother and Teita suspect that there was something 'fundamentally wrong' with me that evening.

Their night-long anxiety triggered off a big family commotion. Meanwhile, I made a fuss that far exceeded my real fears and feelings: it was a cunning nine year old finally winning a major battle against 'safe' Assyrian Protestant family homes.

At this point in my life it is rather difficult for me to figure out which of the two failed me most—today's menopausal memory (or lack of it), or a childhood that I never really had.

Coming of Age

If my early childhood years were formed by being rebellious against my grandmother's, and to a lesser extent, my parents' values, my adolescent years were shaped by the numerous books surrounding me.

It was my father's psychiatry books, which I read in utter secrecy, that troubled me but also widened my horizons. They provided me with the necessary expertise to explain everything to my teenage schoolmates who knew little about the range of human conditions—anxiety, depression, egocentricity, narcissism, phobias and schizophrenia. I understood most of this, but it was specially difficult to explain to my best friends, Mona and Maha, why schizophrenia was considered a mental illness, as almost all family members (especially children), friends and teachers, were diagnosed by us as having at least one or two 'symptoms of schizophrenia'. We spent endless hours laughing hysterically while trying to guess who was schizophrenic:

"Okay. Now first listen to what it means: Schizophrenia means split mind. It comes from two Greek words: schizo which means 'split' or 'divide', and phren which means 'mind'. Now listen carefully to the symptoms and try to diagnose who around us is schizophrenic." I would give my instructions and continue reading:

"The person loses the ability to think clearly, logically and coherently, this makes him have funny beliefs." I stopped reading instantly and screamed: "That must be Grandma!"

"That's Mum," said Mona, seriously.

"That's exactly Dad," giggled Maha.

I continued reading:

"Listen carefully again: 'Schizophrenics hear strange voices, talk to personalities in their minds; they don't like people and have a tendency to stay alone, they also think people are plotting against them.'"

I stopped again and said: "See, it is Grandma, for sure, because she thinks that Arabs and non-Protestants are always plotting against 'us' Protestant Syrians."

Maha interrupted me by saying: "Oh, my God, do you think my five year old sister Nura is schizophrenic? She always hears noises and sees visions. She sees and hears things that don't exist in reality. She imagines things: she imagines out-of-space creatures, she sees flying dogs and unicorns, she also sees walking fish and often talks to them."

Only then did I realise that children's wild imaginations and grown-ups' insanity were symptoms of schizophrenia!

In one session alone, we were able to diagnose at least five or six severe or mild cases of schizophrenia:

Our teacher Nadia who 'doesn't like people' and always screams at students.

My brother George 'who had a tendency to stay all by himself'.

Our neighbour who had a 'split personality' because he had a lover in addition to his wife.

Our friend Karim because he had 'unbalanced emotional reactions such as feeling sad on a happy occasion or happy on a sad occasion'. Karim never enjoyed school parties and often complained that we were talking abut him.

And I, of course, added Bibi who 'acted funny', to the long list.

Dad's book also explained homosexuality. But that I kept to myself as I had difficulty sharing the problematic and confusing information with Maha and Mona. The only time I shared this 'scientific knowledge' with Dad I got into serious trouble.

"Is God a homosexual?" I asked inquisitively. I got a grim look but no answer. It was the only time I recall that Dad was not too proud of my knowledge.

Dad's book read: "Homosexual means of the same sex. Homo is a Greek word which means same and sex is a Latin word." The book also explained how the word homosexual was relatively new. "It first appeared in 1969 in a German pamphlet by the Austrian-born novelist Karl-Maria Kertbeny." But the book had a photograph of an old cup (480 BC) depicting two men making love: Gods Zephyrus and Hyacinthus. Below the photograph was the story of how both Apollo (god of prophecy, music and healing) and Zephyrus (god of soft wind) fell in love with a very handsome and athletic Spartan prince. The two competed for the boy's love but he chose Apollo, driving Zephyrus mad with jealousy. Later, catching Apollo and Hyacinthus throwing a discus, Zephyrus blew a gust of wind at them, striking the boy in the head with the falling discus. When Hyacinthus died, Apollo created the hyacinth flower from his blood."

There were three facts in this that really disturbed me:

First, how come there was more than one God?

Second, how come the God made love to a human?

And third, how come God killed his lover?

This must have shaken my belief in God(s) for a lifetime, and to my attitude to homosexuality for some time; as for the hyacinth, till today, I feel funny whenever I smell one.

The world of Bibi's straight sex out of books turned out to be a necessary first step towards my theoretical fantasy world: of orgasm and oral sex, of sexual fetishism and homosexuality, and of exhibitionism, which led me to scream to my girl friends: "Don't get scared, and don't pay him any attention, that *is exactly* what he wants." But in spite of my theoretical knowledge, we *all* screamed in fear and he had his orgasm.

Jean-Paul Sartre's existentialism drove me away from the ethics of the New World of America, to which my Dad and all my cousins (including Bibi) were aspiring. I was slowly breaking away from Dad as my admiration for Abdul Nasser,

Arab Nationalism and Marxism resulted in heated arguments between me and my pro-McCarthyism father. Albert Camus' 'struggle with absurdity' managed to shed more light on the absurdity of my life, that of a ghettoised minority. I had underlined that *one line* in Camus' *Plague* over and over which read:

> *There were others who rebelled, and whose one idea now was to break loose from the prison-home.*

It wasn't till I was fourteen or perhaps fifteen that my anger at Grandma's cup of coffee was put into context for me by Simone de Beauvoir's 'one is made, not born, a woman'. See, Teita, that's what I meant to say all along. While de Beauvoir's *Second Sex* rid me of superfluous romance (which I don't think I had to begin with), it prepared me *intellectually* to face the essence of love and marriage: sex. I was with my cousin Vanouch in the swimming pool when I spotted blond Vaché with his friend Aram. Having studied de Beauvoir's instructions well, it didn't take me long to express my 'physical attraction' to innocent Vaché as we took long walks along the main boulevards of Damascus for more than a year, sat on isolated benches on the high mountain of Masyoun, and often disappeared into the darkness of the cinema, which I adored.

"We have taken the decision to send you to the American University of Beirut a year earlier," said my father's authoritative voice.

I could see my mother's doubting eyes move between me and Dad.

What was meant as a punishment for a big love affair was

turning out to be an early break away from my prison-home! Turning my back on it all, including my sweet love, Vaché, was a price I was absolutely ready to pay in order to be in cosmopolitan, rebellious Beirut.

"Okay, fine with me," was my agreeable short reply. I was trying hard to avoid discussing the real issue at this urgent parent-daughter summit.

"Is it true what we've been hearing, Flora? You've been alone with him in seclusion, haven't you? This is utterly unacceptable for a girl your age. You've got to promise us, this will have to stop right away."

Simone de Beauvoir, could you please help me with my first, let alone *second, sex?*

I knew I was *forever* on my way out of this ghettoised Assyrian world against which I rebelled totally. While I was on my way to Beirut, the heart of Arab nationalism, all my family members, only a few years later, were on their way to the 'free world'.

I threw myself fearlessly into what seemed then a cosmic infinite world. And with the recklessness (and wisdom) of a seventeen-year old, I turned my back on it all, with absolutely no regrets.

5

Ann

My life started with a military occupation in Japan and will probably end with the one in Palestine, but this time there seems to be no liberation.

San Francisco, 1965

It was with a strong sense of *morality* and *justice* that the frail teenager who appeared in the photograph stood in front of a huge American soldier, one of many, mounting a smart light brown horse whose size, not grace, matched that of his master.

Had it not been for the eviction of elderly Chinese living in a run-down hotel due to be torn down for urban renewal, there would have been many more similarities between the blonde girl and the elegant brunette horse; he was up in the air bending backward while standing on his two back legs; she was up on her toes with wide open arms, her spine bending backwards.

Unlike the stylish horse who had no option but to go along with his western cowboy master, she had taken a nonretractable position against her own government.

Her soft but rather austere appearance was very similar to that of her Swedish pastor grandfather. However, her bohemian life and radical activism contrasted sharply with his German-educated theology, her physician-father's fear of socialised medicine and communism, and the serenity and boredom of the chicken farm on which her mother grew up in Quincy, a tiny village out there in nowhere, in mid-west America.

Maybe she needed the recognition of this world-famous anti-Vietnam war photograph to have her *go* ... for the rest of her life.

But this was not the first time a photograph played a major role in her life.

Basic Instincts, Kyoto 1948

Perhaps it was the inner soul and deep unspoken feelings of her Japanese Nanny, Kiyoko, that instinctively nourished the infant's strong sense of human justice—or was it injustice?

Her love and passionate attachment to her middle-aged Nanny were easily captured in the infant's early black and white photograph. Standing on the terrace in front of her master's house on the American military base of Kyoto, tiny Kiyoko was tenderly holding the one-year-old blonde Ann.

The two beaming smiles on both faces revealed a life-long promise they had already made to one another; only *they*, and probably the little dog which appears in the right-hand corner of the tiny photograph, pushing against Kiyoko's miniature feet, knew what the promise was all about.

57

Could 1948, the year in which the photograph was taken, also the year in which hundreds of thousands of Palestinians were being pushed out of their homeland, be a *prophecy* or an *omen* to a cause to which the infant, some thirty years later, ends up dedicating the rest of her life?

But as had been promised to beloved Kiyoko—first Japan, then Vietnam, then Korea, then ... then ... the path was long and wearisome.

The terrifying events of World War II in the American military base on the Pacific convinced her just-out-of-medical-school father that there must be some less dramatic places that could make use of his newly acquired medical skills; from the military base in Japan to those in Alabama and Texas, and then a few years later, to an air force base south of London.

A few years in the huge walled-off base left five-year-old Ann with a vague, sketchy, child's eye-view memory: a rabbit-hunter huge white cat, bunk beds for her, her younger sister, Martha and brother Tim, also for Jim, her first love, who lived just next door on the base. Some fifty years later she can still remember American built houses, military style, with front yards full of bright yellow and purple pansies, where they all stood watching exciting field days. At home, a little bit shadowed but bright and funny housewife-mother who hardly complained except, once a year, when drunken American generals tried to kiss her every New Year's Eve party. Neither she, nor her even-tempered husband, liked the drunken generals' and colonels' bad behaviour, but the confinement of the air force base and strict military hierarchy left them with little space for grievances.

Unlike Tim and Jim, who always managed to run away from

the base, Ann often got stuck under the barbed wire fence surrounding the gated community. It was her deep love for nature and the nearby woods that made her take the risk of being caught (and salvaged) by the military guards; this also gave her the necessary practice for penetrating nuclear bases, against which she demonstrated later in the Sixties.

The one time she *finally* managed to run away from the internment of the base into the freedom and wilderness of the woods, she found herself face to face with a fox. They stood still, staring at one another, with two small pumping hearts, sharp fox eyes and fox-like eyes. They soon came to terms with one another—each went their own way. This face to face encounter prepared Ann for all future face to face, risky, often dangerous and sometimes life-threatening encounters. Looking back at things fifty-four years later, the encounter with the English fox was perhaps the simplest to handle. It took an intelligent animal and a non-retrieving female child to understand that there was no need to hurt one another; more importantly, they understood that matters could be solved peacefully.

The tamed English landscape, butterflies, 'wild' man-made gardens of her mother's English friends in the small town of Mixford nearby, and the yuppie school for young English ladies in which her Mama *first* enrolled her, all contrasted with the solitude and blandness of the American base; she loved everything that was on the *other side* of that fence: her English school, her English friends, her English teachers, she even liked English meals.

She so much wanted to be part of *this* community that no trace remained of her tendency to run off on her own, doing her own thing, or of her bossiness in the house, especially around Tim and Jim, or for that matter giving Mum advice or terrifying little Martha by telling her there were angels hovering over her bed. None of that could be detected at her beloved English school. Unlike her American hunting pet on the base, *here* she was the teachers' pet. She just wanted them to take her under their wing.

The one American trace that persisted was her eagerness *to be a star,* and in a way she was. Her American mid-west accent made her stand out as different, and so did her remarkable performance at school, particularly her reading abilities; at four she had already learned how to read, and by the age of nine there was hardly a book around that she hadn't read. With numerous displacements to world-wide American military bases, her books became her anchor and her refuge. They also carried her away from base imprisonment to the world of Robin Hood, Pinocchio, Don Quixote, Sherlock Holmes and many others. The vast fields of articulated words and literary fantasies she found herself in had no resonance in her Swedish, mid-western and farmers' family backgrounds. It was with a kind of code, rather than an articulated language, that her family members communicated. The few-words communication code often made her recall her Swedish grandma's story: "In the north of Sweden where we came from, a visit to the nearest neighbour was a few kilometers away. Knock at their door, they would open it, and with hardly a welcoming word a hot cup of coffee would be served. And with almost no more words exchanged the short visit would end." Decoding her family's mode of communication was often as difficult as decoding WWII American air force ciphers.

It was with a great sense of sadness that she left behind the rolling hills of south England and returned to Quincy, Alabama. With a three-child family and a fourth on the way, Dr. Frederickson finally decided there must be a better way to 'see the world'. Though originally a city boy from Chicago, he opted for his wife's little town. Quincy was a normal (as normal as it gets in America) civilian town. Its size, isolation and provinciality were, after all, not that different from the series of military bases where he had spent his married life so far.

As far as teenage Ann was concerned, real life was happening elsewhere, behind the un-drawn boundaries of Quincy. Her childhood experiences had already sharpened her senses, as well as her consciousness, that there were infinite and exciting wider horizons 'out there'. There was an eagerness to be on the other side of the fence. Unlike the rest of her mid-west classmates, she had a strong sense of 'the Other'. In vast America, unlike England, things were not happening in the village next door but thousands of miles away.

One thing was very clear in her mind: "I don't want to be *here*, I want to be *there*," she confided to her best friend, Jenny, as they sat mesmerised watching it all happening on television. But this time there was certainly no friendly and accommodating environment. This time there was: Selma, Alabama, Birmingham, Martin Luther King, the civil rights movement; demonstrators being beaten up, injured or killed. Two *very long* years of high school at Quincy passed with hell breaking loose *out there* before 1965, the year Ann and Jenny finally made it made to the new horizons of Rice University in Houston, Texas.

While piles of revolutionary books were making sense of world matters, Bob Dylan's exhilarating Sixties songs were breaching Ann's basement walls, freeing the seventeen-year old radical and connecting her to a world community of rebels, and to a long list of world issues and liberation movements.

First Vietnam, then Korea, then a long psychedelic summer of love, then anarchism, then Marxism, then a long-distance phone call to student rebels in Burma directly from the occupied president's office, then Angola, then Cuba, then storming and burning a few government offices here and there, then a few visits by the FBI: while some went underground, others shaved and behaved, and Ann decided it was time to take a short fighter's pause and re-examine the world.

With a satisfied smile on her face, her probing eyes moved between the huge map of the world hanging on the wall in her room, the accompanying checklist she kept right next to it, and her Nanny's black and white photograph.

On her map, the liberation green pins indicating freedom were numerous. She had recently pinned the Philippines, Iran, Nicaragua and Chile, green. With a deep sigh she thoroughly examined the *still* remaining three red pins indicating the continuation of colonial rule: one marked South Africa, another marked Ireland and the third, which marked a country whose name had been wiped out from all maps.

After twenty-five years of living in Palestine the big red pin still marks a country whose people and land (not only its name) are still being erased.

Through the labyrinth of Ann's long life, all had been possible except—Palestine.

6

Reem

A Monopoly Game, Jerusalem 1952

I woke up terrified. Shaking, I sat up in bed. It took me a while to realise that *she* was the source of the horrifying noises that woke me up in the middle of the night. I wondered if she too was dying. The reflections of the orange street light on her long untidy white hair, and on the bright red spots visible through the holes of her white crocheted duvet added to my anxiety. I slipped out of bed and went running across the living room seeking the only warmth I ever got from Mum: that of her bed.

It was only a few days earlier that she had decided I should move out of my bedroom—which, so far, I had shared with my older brother, Nadim. "Your bother needs his privacy," she said in her usual aloof tone. He was fourteen, I was eleven. Till the day Mum died she never thought that *I* may also have needed my privacy or, God forbid, have my own desires.

"Mum . . . how do children make it to this world?" She was totally flabbergasted.

With a low restrained voice she replied:

"I'll tell you when you get engaged."

"And what if I don't?"

"In that case, you'll die not knowing."

In fact I never got engaged, and at ninety-one Mum died, her information undisclosed.

Though anti-clerical, Dad, like many honeymooners in the Forties and Fifties took his bride to the Qbeibeh Monastery, only fifteen kilometres away from their home in Jerusalem. The Monastery's lavish garden and the nearby pine and oak forest provided the newlyweds with the desired tranquility and poetic environment.

It was early 1940; she was twenty-eight, he was thirty-five.

They had fallen in love a few years earlier when she went to work in the same bank opposite her family's house.

With a few years of slow, but cumulative, experience of holding her hand, tenderly embracing her, and even kissing her on the cheek, the groom gained the necessary stamina and confidence to perform that night:

"No ... you can't do that! I come from a *good* and a *respectable* family *(min 'Eileh meneeha o muhtarameh)*. No ... we don't do such things," she insisted.

As she was adamant about coming from a good and respectable family, he on his part insisted it was time they had their *own* respectable family. At the end of the shorter-than-planned honeymoon, Rushdi had no choice but to take his bride back to her respectable Mum and Dad: "Once you explain to her the meaning of life, I'll be back to pick her up."

In a week's time or so, he was back. In exactly nine months their first baby, Nadim, was born. Three years later I showed up, and three years after that my younger brother, Jamal. Once every three years seemed to have been the frequency of their love-making. It could have been a *bit* more than three times in more than a decade, but it couldn't have been less. Having by accident seen them once, plus their habit of calling each other *habibi* and *habibti* (my beloved) must have given me the wrong impression. It wasn't until I was five that I realised that Rushdi, not *habibi*, was Dad's real name. The rest I found out in my old age, when I became Dad's true confidante.

Mum's new sleeping arrangements meant I shared a bedroom with my eighty-year old Tante Silvia, but it also meant that I slept in the bed of my beloved Grandma Christina who had just died a few weeks earlier. The three tiny bedrooms in which Dad, Mum and little Jamal; Nadim; Grandma Christina and her sister, Tante Silvia slept, left me with little manoeuvring space to protest against Mum's new sleeping arrangements.

To add to my misfortune, Grandma's death had aggravated Tante Silvia's grimness and glumness. As Dad always said: "Tante Silvia has been out-of-place since she left her tiny village in the south of France a century ago" (meaning the end of the nineteenth century). On her first pilgrimage to the Holy Land Grandma Christina fell in love with Grandpa Najib "a handsome Arab man," she always said in her broken Arabic with a French accent. On her second pilgrimage to Jerusalem she dragged her younger sister along and married her off to the slightly retarded and rather ugly younger brother of her beloved husband, Najib. While Grandma was actively producing thirteen babies, Silvia, who had none, took care of them all.

I often stared at the out-of-focus black and white family photograph on the wall of our living room. In the middle of the photo stood Mum and Dad, very close to one another; Mum's still, outstretched arm held Nadim who stood right next to her, while Dad's strong arm around me almost strangled me. Little squeezed-in Jamal was pushing for a place. On Mum's side was Grandma who sat comfortably on a cane armchair while Tante Silvia, standing on one leg, leaned against its edge.

With Grandma dead Silvia was waiting for her turn. Perhaps that's why she was making those horrifying noises.

As my heartbeats merged with her horrific snores, I made it in the darkness across the living room separating Tante Silvia's bedroom from that of my parents. I took a deep breath the minute I saw a dim light under their shut door. Not to add to the noise level of Tante Silvia's snores, and making sure not to give Mum any excuse to object to my sneaking into the warmth of their bed, I carefully opened their door and quietly, on tip-toe, stepped into their bedroom. I stood there and gasped.

He was bouncing on top of her. She was motionless; her left arm was dangling down her side of the bed while the other was stretched out next to her naked body. He was mumbling. She was speechless. I couldn't figure out what he was saying. I looked for the *knife* in his hand, and all around him, but couldn't find it.

Having no other choice that night, I settled for restless sleep on the living room sofa. Trying hard to shut out the noise around me, I put my hands on my ears and stuck my head under the cushion. Restless and sleepless, I recalled my older schoolmates' intimate whispering:

"On the wedding night, the man (the groom) comes to his woman (the bride) with a knife in his hand and forces her to take off all her clothes and lie naked in bed." My schoolmate was so confident of her knowledge and I was so scared and gullible, that I ran away from all the other schoolmates' sex education. Only then did I realise why Mum was not in a hurry to reveal to me the horrifying fact of the knife.

With the break of dawn I had totally forgotten about Tante Silvia's snores but more than ever, I was mad at Dad.

Up until that day he was my love, my support and my ally. In English I was his Princess; in Arabic I was his *habibti*; in French his *cherie*. Though I was his, much more than Nadim was Mum's, still he wasn't supposed to scare her with a knife.

I was mute for the next two days. No one ... no one, *especially* him, could talk to me.

It took a red coat with a pink fur lining to make up for his crime. "Come with me, my beautiful princess," he sweet-talked me, and hand in hand we went round and round, in and out of all Jerusalem's old city's shops. Once I was bribed and done with, my dream-like shopping spree over, he bought *her* the most gorgeous string nightgown. I was trying hard to make sense of this shopping spree, of my winter pink fur coat, her summer nightgown and Dad's missing knife.

The Birthday Girl, Autumn 1961

"No one ... no one, can ever ... ever *possess* or *touch* my *only* daughter ... do *you* understand? Now get out of my house ...!" The three of us, Nadim, Sami and I, stood still, terrified. We were totally flabbergasted by his out-of-the-blue outrage.

Sami went white as Dad came close to him and, from one inch away, stared him in the eye while his screams continued: "Get out of here before I throw you off the balcony . . . do you hear me? Not over my dead body will I allow the son of a drunkard and a gambler to come near my *only* daughter!" Dad had totally lost it. I stood there mesmerised. I hadn't so far ever seen such hostility from Dad towards anyone, let alone my brother's closest friend. Nadim and Sami had dropped out from the scene, Nadim for a few hours and Sami for quite a while.

I was celebrating my fourteenth birthday. All invitees had left when Sami, to my utter happiness, suggested he stay behind to play Monopoly. The three of us were sitting around the dining table playing, when Dad walked in the door. I instantly tried to distance myself, my body, away from Sami's, but was one second too late. Dad must have seen our legs under the table.

He realised instinctively that this was not exactly an innocent game of Monopoly.

For a few minutes I was hostage to Dad's emotions and his unprecedented explosion. Mum and Tante Silvia, whose card game had been interrupted, came in from the balcony and stood there speechless, waiting for my father's torrent to end.

"Help her gather her belongings! I am taking her to Monastery's boarding school right now."

I was hoping Mum would intervene on my behalf and convince Dad otherwise, but since she has never stood up to him, in less than half an hour I was with him, dragging my feet as he dragged my belongings towards the boarding section of my school. A short walk, just before sunset, in the crooked alleys of the old city brought us right in front of Sister

Antoinette's office. I was instructed to stay behind while he disappeared into her office. I had no clue what kind of deal was struck between the two of them, but one thing I definitely recall was the shiver that ran down my spine as Sister Antoinette reassured Dad, saying:

"Don't worry ... you go away now ... we shall take her in today and keep her safely with us for *the rest of her life.*"

I burst into hysterical tears as I saw Dad turn his back on me.

Was he affirming his absolute monopoly over me by giving me up to God?

The ten minute distance separating home from school became my longest emotional break from Dad for years to come.

I couldn't figure out the main reason for my night-long weeping—was it the thwarted longing for a first and unconsummated love story, or the terrible memories it brought back of early childhood separation?

When I was four, Mum got very sick and couldn't take care of my two brothers and me. Nadim was sent to my beloved Grandma Azizeh in Bethlehem, while I was brought to this same Monastery where my mother's sister, Tante Nicole, lived.

I recall vividly her taking me by the hand along the same path between home and Monastery, and into the vast and dark dining room. My cold legs were dangling below the wooden bench as I leaned on her warm body. She asked me to sit up straight as the big Sister in a black dress bounced a laminated bowl right in front of me on the bare table. Lukewarm drops of water spilled on the table, while a few drops splashed on my chin. I lowered my neck to the deep bowl only to see pieces of carrot drowning in dirty brown water. I was instantly nauseated as my stomach turned. "Eat your dinner," was the godly command of the big Sister, and the small command of Tante Nicole. Refusing to do so started a series of punishments that never ended: for three consecutive days, carrots were offered for breakfast, lunch, afternoon light snacks, and dinner. That wasn't all: right after the disgusting dinner, I was accompanied through the darkness of the Monastery with my aunt: once more I lugged myself behind, staring at the countless fluorescent big eyes placed along the dark and gloomy corridor. In no time I learnt my alphabets so as to figure out what was written below them: GOD IS WATCHING YOU.

To this very day carrots, big black eyes, nuns in black and religion classes bring back the same shivers.

One thing I never really understood: why were nuns so much into punishment and so anti-fun? If caught laughing in class, one was made to stand for hours on one leg or kneel with both legs on a bed of pebbles. Perhaps being so close to God made punishment an acceptable mode of behaviour.

But at fourteen, with a big romance waiting for me outside, I did all it took for me to be released from the boarding section of the school and get back home.

For years to come, with much love, obsession and sometimes deception, I succeeded in striking the right balance between Dad's true monopoly, and Sami's Monopoly game.

Paris, Summer 1967

At last, at nineteen, I was on my way to study in everybody's dream city: Paris.

slim with a sweet face and attractive piercing little eyes, the other was tall with a big moustache. Totally focused, I sat there trying to comprehend the half-Arabic-half-French new terminologies: bourgeois, working class, leftist, internationalist, Marxist-Leninist, Maoist, unionist—and Vietnam. From an extremely long list, perhaps only Zionism, Palestine, Israel and the PLO sounded familiar. Though most heated discussions went over my head, day by day, I was getting interested in their issues, high on their (and soon my) smoke, totally hooked to their (and soon my) political activism, and rather comfortable around their (not mine) bohemian way of life.

In reality, it was my deliberately cultivated coquettish appearance, my innocence and, above all, my French passport that made me ideal for the many shuttle 'missions' between Paris and Jerusalem. Until one trip in 1977 when I was arrested, investigated and ultimately deported. I vividly recall every word of my last intimate talk with Dad: he and I had been chatting through the night till the early morning hours of my deportation, which I had concealed from him until the Israeli jeep and soldiers pulled up and banged loudly at our courtyard's iron gate. They pulled me away from home, away from Jerusalem, and away from Dad who died two months after I was deported.

The life, and the assassination by Mossad, of the sweet face with attractive piercing eyes of the PLO representative in Paris, ruled over my life forever.

7

Luisa

(Honorary Mention)

*Till today I can't tell which of the two smells shaped my life as
a trade unionist: the smell of my aunt's apple caramel or the
smell of the poor factory workers' minestrone?*

Villadossola, Italy 1945

It *all* fell into place the minute he explained: "Once the male
bee fertilises the female queen he goes away and dies. He has
performed his duty and function in life successfully. Once the
female bee gives birth to her little ones, she has also fulfilled
her role, duty and function, hence she also dies. We call this a
complete life-cycle."

I was totally mesmerised by what my elementary teacher
had just said. I didn't quite understand what fertilise meant,
but it didn't really matter as the rest of the story made
complete sense. That's what it is after all: natural and
complete!

Dad had gone away to the mountains (now I know, after
he had fertilised the queen). There he died with the rest of the

Partisans. People say thirty-three of them died while the rest took refuge in the high mountains and later sought refuge in Switzerland. Could Mum have been the queen of the newly-formed Italian Republic, partigiana dell' Ossola? All the villagers and teachers in our village (Villadossola) were extremely proud that ours was *the first* Italian republic to be declared in October 1944. It lasted 13 days before the fascists came and all the men, including Dad, ran away.

Now I understand that killing my mother was a natural act completing the teacher's 'life-cycle'. Since Mum, like Dad, had also fulfilled her 'duty', 'role' and 'function' by giving birth to the three of us: myself, Elario and Francesco, my two younger brothers—it was time for her to die.

Only now, looking back, have I understood. Too young to have a teacher, Elario and Francesco displayed no signs of anxiety about their mother being killed.

What baffled me was little Francesco's lack of concern about his beloved Mum. All her life, Mum never stopped bragging about her blond and beautiful baby. Elario and I, both ugly, as Mum always said, nourished a life-time bond.

It was Mum who prevented me from throwing baby Francesco into the kitchen hearth when he was a few months old. I was getting sick and tired of him and Mum crying and screaming at the same time, all the time. From day one, when he was born, Francesco cried constantly. His crying was more like shrieking screams that began and never ended. As Mum carried him around the house and nervously patted him, she also cried: partly because Dad was gone, partly because Francesco never stopped screaming, and partly because she hardly had any milk or food to feed him.

"Mum, why don't we throw Francesco into the fire, this way his screams will stop and so will yours. Dad is gone, there's no one around to see ..."

In a fraction of a second, Mum grabbed me by my ponytail and swung me left, right and centre. Then started slapping me on the face, picked up her slippers and hit me all over. As was often the case, once I had fallen to the floor she would sit on top of me and start breathing heavily. It wouldn't be long before her screaming and yelling would flip into words of love and care: "You're my love, you're my darling, and you're my queen ... you know well, you're my everything." Then she would hug me and start weeping quietly. Having gone through this drama too many times in my life, I learnt how to resist her emotional oscillations and manipulation; I would look her in the eye, determined not to cry ever. And always say the same words: "I hate you, Mum. I want to kill you."

Having expressed my true feelings towards her, I would run into my room, lock the door and escape out of the window into the vastness of the high mountains. A few hours later, I would come back across the river and along its west bank, stop at the little shrine and utter a few words to Madonna. She understood me very well. Promised to help me kill my mother.

I took my two brothers into my bedroom, clicked the door shut, and revealed the intricate details of my secret plot to kill her. Being boys, they seemed to instantly and instinctively understand the need to kill.

Even though it was all my doing, I was a bit troubled by the idea, but could not, and did not want to go back on it:

"We (meaning I) should ask Mum to accompany us to the

mountains in order to look for Dad's corpse. Mum should come with us as she's the only who knows what Dad had on the night he went with the other fighters. People say it's important to remember the colour of his shirt so as to identify the corpse. They also said how difficult it was to identify Partisans' corpses, because most wore blue or white shirts and grey or navy blue trousers. I once overheard Uncle Giovanni explain to Mum how corpses were preserved in the snow on the mountains, but Mum wept even more as Dad had disappeared on a hot summer day; so much more reason for Mum to accompany us to the mountains."

All was set and under control. While we waited for her to come back from her work at the textile factory nearby, we did a few more rounds of the 'giggling drills' or, more accurately, 'no laughing drills'. These were anti-fascist disciplinary exercises which entailed giggling without laughing. I explained the fascists' cruel methods of extracting information from Partisans to my two brothers: they would keep giggling at us, and we would laugh so much till we collapsed and named the Partisans and their whereabouts. These drills could also be useful, particularly for Francesco, in plotting against Mum. I kept the thought to myself as Francesco and Elario giggled and laughed.

I went to have a look at Mum's black and white photograph which *she* had hung in my room: she was standing in a funny studio next to a square table which had exactly the same shape as her head. Her slightly wavy hair also had a square cut just below the ears. Her light beige vest with big buttons in front accentuated her bosom, while her long, dark-grey, tight skirt accentuated her derrière. I always told her that when she stood straight in her high-heel shoes, her bosom reached the

Romanesque church and her derrière, the other church—they were at two opposite ends of our village.

Mum loved her body and I hated mine.

The minute she hung her coat and started complaining, as usual, about the terrible 'this' and the awful 'that' at the factory, I gathered my courage and said in an eldest sister's commanding tone:

"*Mum*, you must come with us, we want to look for Dad's corpse in the mountains."

"Cara Luisa ... *per favore*, don't you *ever* say *that* again, it's a bad omen, no one is certain that Dad has died, we should all pray that he comes back safe and sound. Anyway, Elario and Francesco are too young for this kind of talk."

I could see how indifferent and resigned both Elario and Francesco were about being excluded from the plot. I nodded to give them comfort and reassurance, which they seemed not to need. I knew I could do it alone. Perhaps it would be even better without them—I would be in total control.

Mum and I kept walking up the hill until we reached the very top of the mountain. Once we were at the steep cliff (which I had checked out many times before), I pushed her down, watched her fly and before she hit the big rocks down in the valley, I came running down. I could also fly. Though absolutely thrilled, I didn't forget to pass by and thank Madonna: "Had it not been for your help, I wouldn't have been able to do it all by myself." I lit one of the many candles lying around and ran back home.

"Why so late, Luisa, where have you been all this time?" As I set foot inside the house, I heard Mum's voice from the kitchen.

"I went fishing with the neighbours' kids, I won the competition."

"How many times do I have to tell you not to take forks from the kitchen, people fish with nets and rods … we're hardly left with any."

Since there was hardly any food at home, I thought forks could be better used.

"And where are *all* the winner's fish?" Mum asked jokingly.

Except for Aunt Marisa and Uncle Giovanni, none of our relatives or friends had much food. All we ate was potatoes, potato peels and bread. Mum would scold me whenever I drank Francesco's milk, "Your baby brother needs the milk to grow up," she would yell.

I'll never forget the big row I caused between Mum and Aunt Marisa. I had gone to play with my cousin Bianca. As we ran round and round the garden of their huge house, I smelt a delicious aroma seeping out of their kitchen window. After a few rounds of the house, I could no longer resist the temptation. Pretending I had to go to the toilet, I sneaked into the kitchen and flipped open the oven door. Saliva filled my mouth the minute I set eyes on rows of apples, sliced into halves, with caramel melting on top of them. As quickly as I could, I picked up two, one in each hand, ran into Aunt Marisa's bedroom and slipped under her bed. I had burnt fingers and tongue before the caramel cooled off, and before Bianca and her Mama came looking for me.

I never could figure out which feelings took hold of me most: the yummy taste of the caramel apple that stayed with me all my life, or my embarrassment as Aunt Marisa ordered me to come out from under her bed, and my poor mother's refusal to believe that her child would ever steal food.

That was to be the *one* story Mum kept repeating to Dad when he finally returned home a year or two later. Neither Mum nor Aunt Marisa recognised the necessity of forgetting this story for the sake and dignity of a growing child. Dad often turned a deaf ear: partly because of guilt at leaving behind a wife and three unfed kids, partly because he was drunk, and partly because he had long learnt not to take sides for or against his neurotic wife, and the wife of his only relatively rich brother.

With a kind, hard-working, drunken Dad, things were slowly improving around the house and also around Mum's factory, where we spent seven exciting months which *truly* changed my life. I vividly recall the day Mum came home and took us children to join all the families of her striking textile workers. It must have been May of 1951. As she went around the house, picking up a few things here and there, I heard her tell Dad with unprecedented confidence: "There will be a textile workers' strike for as long as it takes these *idiots* to go back on their *stupid* and *irresponsible* decision to close the factory and lay off all the workers."

I was so excited at missing school that I immediately helped her gather Elario and Francesco's clothes. Off we all went hand-in-hand to the factory. We laid our things neatly on the many mattresses spread all over the gigantic hall right next to the huge machines. Once settled, I ordered Elario and Francesco to stay still and behave, and followed Mum to her union meeting. Being eleven years old I was given many important tasks; most of all helping others cook the huge minestrone. I asked if it was the same huge pot that Dad and his Partisan friends used in the mountains, but no one seemed to know. When I brought a chair and climbed up to look inside, I heard Comrade Paolo say: "Be careful not to fall in, Luisa."

Till today I can't tell which of the two smells shaped my life as a trade unionist: the smell of my Aunt's apple caramel or of the poor factory workers' minestrone?

I stood on a high table in order to watch the trade union leader, Teresa Bertenotti; she herself stood on an even higher stage holding a huge megaphone which amplified her incomprehensible words and long sentences. It was the size of her megaphone, the volume of her high-pitched voice that made me join in the applause of Mum's excited colleagues. One thing I was sure about as I watched her animated movements and features: being a clever woman and as ugly as Teresa Bertenotti, *I* could also become a trade unionist.

At the thought of this, I clapped even more loudly.

Seven months passed by before we were all sent back home; Mum, like most others in Villadossola, no longer had a job to go to.

It was in the same striking red dress which I wore to school when Stalin died in 1954, that I left home and escaped to Bologna. I was thirteen yeas old when I started my first job as a trade unionist.

Part Two

New Blood

I didn't want to admit to youthful Yara that some CRIME members, not all of course, have lost the ability to dwell on specific topics. Five or six years after starting CRIME (whose members had, without admitting it, become post-menopausal by now), it *finally* decided to inject some 'new blood', zest and excitement into it.

'Not necessarily menopausal but at least younger, wilder, with a good sense of humour and a bit of sex, of course,' were the instructions put out by central CRIME. That's how we ended up inviting not only theatrical Rana, but physically striking Maya and bubbly Fadia. However, considering her gorgeous looks and her level of activity, Yara will probably have to wait a decade or so more.

I didn't yet want to disclose to a non-party member that some CRIME members—of course, not all—are totally losing it:

"Yes ... yes, I know exactly what you mean, Suad; one's mind becomes like a skipping disc; it loses some parts while *anxiously* and *obsessively* repeating others; I also experience those fractions of seconds, particularly while driving, when I don't know exactly where I am and how to get to my destination. That's minor; the real problem is when *you* totally lose control; I often find myself screaming my head off, not only at my husband, which is understandable, but also at my very close friends and work colleagues. Sometimes I am so outraged I can easily commit a crime against someone, and of course you know who that *one* is!" Aida cracked a nervous laugh and continued obsessively: "Yes, I know . . . I know, Suad, I am *also* certain that my husband is having an affair, in your case probably with a young and scholarly university student, and in my case, with a young and beautiful member of the International Solidarity Group. I am sure he is having an affair with one of them; you feel it, you know it, but somehow can't prove it, or probably don't want to prove it . . ." another anxious laugh.

At this point I was no longer sure whether Aida was referring to my husband or hers.

Aida's mumbling continued: "The unfortunate thing, Suad, is that I have become hostile, not only towards Maher, but also towards *all* young and attractive women around him, and believe me, darling, there are many! I often feel like a devil, or a monster, around them. Of course, the loss of sleep and of sex doesn't really help . . ."

Thanks God, I've never lost sleep, I thought to myself.

More than any other member of CRIME (except Varda, of course) Aida has been *truly* menopausal for two years; she had manifested *all* possible emotional, psychological as well as physical symptoms; a medical doctor herself, she knew them all and went through them one by one. Not only loss of sleep and of sex but also loss of hormones, loss of calcium, loss of breath, nightmares, hot flashes, sweating, dryness, including in the eyes, osteoporosis, and I noticed lately, loss of confidence ... Her losses seem to be many, except weight and the number of cigarettes she continues to smoke.

"I don't know about you, Suad, but I've started feeling that Maher runs away from home; he's either working late in his office or on a plane to somewhere else. At least you don't have children; *I* have to take care of Maya and Marwan, I am basically their driver, I have to take care of the house, the shopping, look after my sick mother, and his of course, all in addition to my terribly demanding job. Maher does not lift a finger at home; he comes late, complains he has had an impossible day, trying to convince stupid Fatah about this, and the more stupid Left about that ... he then eats in five minutes, collapses in front of the television, flip ... flip ... flip through tens of television channels before his snores override those of the television. I tell you, Suad, I have become s-o-o-o resentful ... really ... as far as I am concerned *he ... is ... good ... for ... nothing.*" There was nervous laughter at both ends this time.

And as she herself said: her mind was beyond doubt 'like a skipping disc which loses some parts while anxiously and obsessively repeating others'.

Realising just how menopausal Aida had become, I helped her end the conversation:

"Okay, Aida ... I've got to go now. I promise to call Majdi and make the necessary reservation and arrangements for our dinner."

"Don't forget, Suad, VIP room at Darna Restaurant on

87

Wednesday February 24. Okay?" I heard her repeat as I quickly hung up before she went at it again.

It wasn't long after that *I* started *anxiously* and *obsessively* reflecting on what Aida had just said: all along I had thought that Salim was running away from his mother, being aloft on a plane most of his life. Now, since she passed away a couple of years ago, I just noticed that his travel patterns haven't really changed.

Have I been menopausal all my life? I asked myself.

I picked up the phone and called Darna Restaurant. It rang once or twice, when I suddenly remembered that I had forgotten to put out the fire under the stuffed chicken. I replaced the receiver and dashed towards the kitchen when I stumbled over Salim's black shoes lying in the middle of the living room. I cursed him, picked them up, and went to put them at the bottom of his closet. The minute I opened the door, I remembered that I had wanted to put it in order for days. I pulled out all his jumbled up clothes, turned round and placed them on our bed. A few minutes later the doorbell rang. I left everything and went to open the door. As soon as I saw Mohammad, the office assistant, who never ever comes without previous notice, I was alerted.

"What is it, Mohammad?"

"Sorry, boss (*m'allimti*), but Fatin sent me to remind you that you have given an appointment to an Italian journalist who has been waiting for you in the office for a while now. Fatin says you forgot to write it in her Agenda, as you had both agreed you would," said Mohammad in his rather polite and sort of low and shy voice.

"Oh, my God ... I'd totally forgotten! But how come she

The excitement of it all and the great sense of freedom made it difficult for me to reciprocate Dad's flood of tears as he hugged me goodbye at Amman's airport.

Overexcited, I could hardly sleep. I woke up with the early yellow sun rays to face my very first day in Paris.

After only a few hours of that same day, June 6, I had to face another new reality:

The 1967 War had just started.

It took a day in Paris for me to realise one never really leaves home.

With a heavy heart and a load of worries about the destiny of Dad, Mum, young Jamal, my friends, my relatives, and my beloved Jerusalem which had fallen into Israeli hands, lonely, I endlessly wandered along the grand boulevards of Paris. For weeks and months to come, I would sit in the parks trying to grasp what had befallen us.

With a respectable family background and a limited (schoolmates') sex education, I decided it was time to marry my beloved Sami who had made it to Milan two years earlier.

In exchange for the letter I sent informing Dad that I was getting married to his rival, in no time I found him right there on my doorstep, in Paris. After fierce battles over my lover's father's whisky bottles and a huge commotion which went on for a few long days, Dad and I parted with swollen red eyes and heavy hearts.

It was only a week or two later that I received a family photograph: they all stood in line with long miserable faces, Mum in a long black dress, Dad and young Jamal with black ties, declaring the death of the daughter they once had.

I cried and cried for hours and days to come.

It only took one plate of Spaghetti Bolognese soaked in tomato sauce for me to decide I could no longer bear the terrible noise and disgusting sounds produced by its hungry eater. I stood up, turned my back and walked out of Sami's life for the rest of mine.

With little money in my pocket, I was once again destined for a monastery: an English one this time. It was a university friend of mine, an American priest, who offered me a room in return for my (non-existent) Arab cooking skills.

My so-far protected life and work around the home and the two monasteries of my life contrasted sharply with the sudden exposure I had, assisting a social worker with the deprived and marginalised. My work with poverty-stricken drunks, drug addicts, prostitutes and the countless number of pregnant young girls, took me to a harsh and ugly world which had absolutely no relation to the idealised Paris to which I had come.

Having seen a photograph of my father among other men in an Israeli jeep in a Swiss journal, and having my sixteen-year old brother arrested with his two best friends, threw me completely off balance. Being politically naïve, like the rest of my ex-family members, I ultimately sought help from my activist Jerusalem friend, Marwan.

The same evening I found myself in a café in a cloud of Gitane smoke emanating from heavy cigarettes and aroma pipes. For one reason or another, all of Marwan's friends were unshaven; a few had goatees, others had thick moustaches, but most had bushy beards and long untidy hair. The political arguments and analysis were mostly between two rather intense men. Both had round eye-glasses: one was hasn't reminded me? And why didn't she call instead of sending you all this way?"

Mohammad looked at me and a soft smile broke out on his lips before he replied: "Well . . . she tried many times, but your line has been busy for quite a while now."

"Strange!" I say and turn around to find that I had left the receiver lying on the small table. As I put it back in its proper place, I remembered I had to call Darna Restaurant, and so as not to forget again I immediately dialled their number:

"Hi, Majdi, can you book us your VIP room for dinner tomorrow? You're going to have some gorgeous CRIME women over."

"Prime women?" enquired Majdi.

"No, CRIME women," I corrected him.

"*Allah Yustur* . . . God forbid, what crime?"

"No . . . no . . . relax, Majdi, CRIME is . . . ." and I explained to him what CRIME stood for.

"Well, Suad, you never know . . . We may end up with two crimes: one tomorrow and another the day after tomorrow," said an amused Majdi, referring to Election Day, and continued: "From now on, I may have to start calling the VIP room upstairs the Harem Room in anticipation of the election results."

"Well, you never know! We've got to practise *just in case,*" I replied.

We both laughed at what we *then* thought was a cute *joke.*

I did not want to alert Majdi that he was about to get, if not the youngest, at least the wildest, the loudest and perhaps the craziest group of women in town, even compared to the Friends' School teenage clientele of his other restaurant,

Angelo's. Really speaking, Majdi opened this chic Darna Restaurant so as to separate the unbearably noisy teenage hamburger-fried potatoes-and-ketchup eaters from older, supposedly more sophisticated, mature and certainly more boring diners.

I didn't want to scare Majdi by telling him that, at least for five or six years now, every time the expanding CRIME membership stepped into a Ramallah restaurant (and Thanks God, there are many) for our menopausal dinners which take place every few months, all other customers would be totally entertained, as well as embarrassed, by our screams and our laughter, but mostly by our tantalising *topics*. It wouldn't be long before most, if not all, the restaurant's curious waiters would be serving our huge table. With a few local Taybeh beers and a few bottles of Chilean wine, we would soon be like a magnet, the centre of attention. If chairs were not openly turned around in our direction, heads would be tilted and necks stretched towards us: all seem to be quietly eavesdropping on our version of 'Sex in the City', which has been omitted from this book.

At Long Last

Darna Restaurant, February 24, 2006

I parked my car right next to the Darna sign which reads:

"*The Best French-Palestinian Gourmet Cuisine in the Most Quiet and Serene Atmosphere.*"

Only Palestinians are capable of such *exaggeration*. The overcooked, charcoal-like barbecued meat served at Darna has absolutely no relation to the stream of blood oozing out of a French Steak Tartare.

Right in front of Darna were parked a few dark Mercedes armoured jeeps and many other fancy cars. Some belonged to CDs (not music, Corps Diplomatique), PNA (Palestinian National Authority or what has been left of it), and IEO (International Election Observers). I don't know why, but these black cars with dark windows remind me of funeral cars which, as a child, scared me to death.

Around each car stood a number of international and local security men, almost all in dark navy blue suits, white shirts, tiny microphones behind their ears, and dark glasses (way after sunset). For one reason or another, most Palestinians associate these glasses with Israeli secret intelligence. Their well-built bodies and grim facial expressions gave the young security men the *aura* they wanted: 'We are in total control.' Whenever I see security men, I wonder, control of what? Yes, control over other security men. They and the exaggerated restaurant sign: "The Most *Quiet* and *Serene* Atmosphere" also reminded me that I hadn't actually been here for quite a while.

It was a cool summer evening when the laid-off, ex-security 'officers' (referred to by most people as *zu'ran,* gangsters), expressed their economic despair, hence their anger and dissatisfaction with the new head of the Palestinian Authority, who had been 'advised' by the American Administration to implement a new policy of re-structuring security apparatuses. But they also meant indirectly to demonstrate their power and ability to impose protection money (*khawah*) on restaurant and shop owners. Shooting, mostly in the air, from their F16 rifles, they went around the town vandalising most restaurants and breaking shop windows. Being a symbol of those who have, as opposed to those who have not, Darna was badly vandalised; hooded gangsters stormed in, shattered the glass of its huge French windows, snatched the white tablecloths with abundant, delicious *mezze* plates, elegant juice, arak and wine glasses, broke the stylistic wooden furniture, shot bullets into the kitchen's huge shiny fridges and aluminium equipment, and left its chic clientele lying flat on their protruding bellies. The day after, a stream of anti-gangster, but also anti-authority (or lack of it) people went around in support of restaurants and shop owners. The flying bullets of the evening left behind some bloodstains and certainly robbed the restaurant of its 'quietness' and 'serenity'. But being a minor incident in our over-eventful lives, I had forgotten all about it.

At the main entrance of the restaurant stood many 'Chiclets boys': "Please … please, *khalto* (aunty) buy from me," said one who came up close, pressing his body against mine. To free myself, I bought four Made in China Chiclets. In no time I was surrounded by the other five. Soon there was a chorus: "Please … please … please buy from me, too."

I was trying to think up an anti-Chiclets-boy strategy when I spotted Miss Lina, my Italian teacher. She was standing right next door in front of her house. Perfect. I rushed to greet her:

"*Buona sera, sur Lina,*" I said proudly, in my Neapolitan-Hebron southern accent.

"*Buona sera, Suad, come sati?*" replied my teacher in old-fashioned Romano.

"*Bene, grazie,*" I said. So far so good. As long as there was no *participio passato* (past participle) in the grammar. I was searching for more Italian words to impress my teacher but found none. So I concluded our conversation by saying: "*Buona notte, Miss Lina.*"

"*Buona notte, cara,*" she replied. Cara, for those of you whose Italian is not as good as mine, means dear. Perhaps you would feel better if you knew that I have spent the last six years studying my *Instant Italian* book which says: 35 minutes a day—in six weeks you'll speak Italian.

Almost everyone in Ramallah knows Miss Lina and Miss Racy, both of whom have been working and living in Ramallah for the last forty-six years. Miss Racy's broken Arabic and amusing accent make me feel I am doing pretty well—I still have forty years to go.

I decided Chiclets boys were less stressful.

I climbed the restaurant's three wide steps. As I walked into a puddle of water from the overflowing fountain, I saw Reem, Jamileh and Flora. They were standing right under the dark brown kitsch ceramic murals over the fountain.

"I wonder how Mahmoud (referring to the world-famous poet, Darwish) feels about having his poetry placed on such terrible art work," said Reem.

"I don't think they could have used it without his permission," replied Flora. But we had to stop being art critics the minute we heard the joyful tones of the restaurant owner: "Right up to the Harem Room," said Majdi playfully as he came out to welcome us. It wasn't long after that Majdi left us and went to chat with the more important clients he had that pre-Election day.

As always, Majdi stood in the long and wide lobby which connected the three main spaces of his restaurant: on the right was the formal Banana Hall (referring to the huge banana trees in the covered greenhouse) where all the monkeys dined. Sorry, I mean where all government officials, diplomats, NGOs, private companies and banks clientele, as well as bourgeois Ramallah families (with screaming kids) sat. To the left was the semi-enclosed elegant terrace overlooking perhaps the only remaining semi-chic neighbourhood among the monstrous newly constructed high-rise buildings of Ramallah. The average age of the terrace clientele was at least twenty years younger than that of the Banana Hall's: here were groups of single men, single women, first rendezvous young lovers, and hubble-bubble (*argieleh*) smokers.

It was also here that live music performances took place during the thirty (or twenty-nine) long evenings and nights of Ramadan. The marathon of Ramadan breakfasting, dinners (*iftar*) should, if not yet, be included in the Guinness Book of Records. It takes a maximum of ten minutes for hundreds of clients to gulp down record amounts of food. Those who truly fast, and the majority of us who pretend to fast, strategically located ourselves around the five-meter long buffet table (and later around the many sweets tables); we would wait there anxiously for the *athan* prayers declaring the end of a long and taxing day of fasting. Whoops ... mounds of rice, meat, chicken, cooked yogurt, shish kebab, pasta, lasagna, cooked vegetable, pastry, roasted mutton, you name it, disappeared, in addition to a huge salad bar and all sorts of sweet dishes that filled two or three round tables. Then in less than half an hour, the musicians would be playing to protruding stomachs, half-open eyes, screaming kids, all in the thick of cigarette and cigar smoke. If anything, Darna has to be complimented for being able to manage such frantically hungry crowds. I say that because I have in the past been witness to some Ramallah restaurant scenes (without mentioning names) during Ramadan *iftar*(s) where some clients were almost stampeded by fasting crowds.

Up the long stairs taking us to the VIP room and the 'lovers' bar,' we went.

As the three CRIME members stood on the upper terrace talking to PLO veteran, Bassam Abu Sharif and others, I hurriedly went to check on how the Harem Room and our menopausal dinner-table looked.

To my utter surprise, all other G7 CRIME members, except for Aida and the three newly acquired ones, had already made it there. Even Ruth who had to come *all the way* from Jerusalem was present (I say *all the way*, because in Palestine we no longer measure distances by kilometers, but by the number of checkpoints and number of hours you have to wait).

I went around greeting them all.

In the middle of the white tablecloth was an amateurish red and white carnation flower arrangement. Around it were placed numerous white plates, silver cutlery and big water, and smaller wine, glasses. The navy blue serviettes contrasted sharply with the red velvety dining chairs which matched the velvety curtains of the windows overlooking the Banana Hall. The austerity of the setting made me have second thoughts about reserving this VIP room, but it was too late to change. Somehow, I always had a strong sense of responsibility for organising our menopause dinners and so acquired the nickname 'Commandant'. I was anxiously pacing in and out of the Harem Room waiting for Aida, Maya, Rana and Fadia. Having waited for more than ten minutes, I decided to calm down; went back into the room and settled into the empty chair in the middle of the table.

Animated, sexy Ola was talking to voluptuous anti-sex Luisa. Both seemed to be over-excited. Ex-dancer, delicate Ruth was seeking one of those difficult explanations from angel-like Ann, and they seemed to be resolving complex political issues calmly. Tiny Reem, silent, with a cigarette in her hand, was absorbed in her own thoughts while staring into space. Flora was describing the details of the last novel she had read at length to patiently-listening Jamileh. Varda seemed to be bored already or was perhaps waiting for Aida, so that they could compare notes or the latest on post-menopause.

As everyone chatted with everyone else, the many young, and some handsome, waiters in black and white costumes came in and out of the room taking drinks orders. Soon they arrived with the menus, went around the table and stood for a while before they succeeded in getting the attention of the over-chatty crowd. Then the 'little performance' of ordering the food started. As is often the case, each one held a menu, examined it carefully, closed it, put it aside, looked up, and then one person normally said (in this case Jamileh): "Shall we order mixed grill and *mezze*?" "Yes ... what a good idea ... but not too much food," came the response (in this case from Ann and Flora). One thing I have never really understood: why do we (and the waiters) always have to go through this little performance before we order exactly the same dish? You may think I am exaggerating, but wait till you're invited to a restaurant in Palestine.

Perhaps this sociological phenomenon needs a bit of explanation. Could it be that at one point in history, eating out was quite festive and only grilled meat was appropriate for this rare event? Even now, when we go to restaurants quite frequently, the charade persists. As the table was being piled with tens of small *mezze* plates, I looked around. Aida, who had initiated it all, was still missing. I asked around and Ann with her quiet voice assured me: "Yes ... yes, Aida is on her way, I just talked to her, she had totally forgotten about the dinner."

"That's menopause, and that is exactly why we have invited new members," I said.

Sure enough, Aida arrived in no time, came in hurriedly and her many apologies rushed in before her. As she settled in, I spotted Maya from a distance.

Not until Maya, a new, pre-menopausal member, dashed into Darna did I—and probably other CRIME members—realise what *younger* and *wilder* really meant.

"*Don't* tell me you're also part of *that* group!" From a distance I could hear Majdi's high-pitched note of disappointment. "What a waste to send a woman like you to the Harem Room upstairs!"

I must admit that I was more troubled (never jealous) by Majdi's flirtatious comments to Maya than by the possibility of Hamas wining the election.

Eventually Maya came into the room. Her skin-tight orange pants, which matched her long and wavy orange hair perfectly, made me sympathise with Hamas' obsession with covering women up. Maya's accentuated features—big brown eyes, voluptuous lips, and neat plastic-surgically operated nose (which troubled her throughout her childhood), added to her wildness, attractiveness and powerful presence. There is something about Maya's looks and mannerisms that give the impression that she is in total control of everything in her life: the tens of architects, engineers and employees working under her command as head of the construction department, her three young daughters, as well as her second husband, if not the first.

Rana's unfulfilled stage aspirations manifested themselves in her theatrical entry into the room which was even more dramatic than that of Maya. After screaming a big "Hi, everybody, *keefkun* (how are you)?" in her exaggerated Lebanese and American accent, Rana carefully threw her brown mink coat on a nearby couch and went around kissing those of us who had, for a while, been sitting around the long table with a sort of last minute flower arrangement. Her model-like criss-cross steps made us admire her beautiful low-cut striking green dress in Ramallah's cold February. However, not being able to tell whether the coat of the late Arafat's adopted daughter was real or false mink, made me recall why most people accused him and the Palestinian Authority, particularly the 'returnees' (*il 'aideen*) of corruption.

Age-wise, Rana belonged to the pre-menopausal new CRIME: 'younger, wilder with a good sense of humour'. However, growing up in Beirut and working closely with Arafat in Tunis, made her share many experiences with our post-menopausal members. In a way, Rana is the link between the older and the younger, and between the 'returnees' and the 'locals', in addition to having a really conspiratorial 'crime' character.

As one of the hundreds of thousands exiled Palestinians (who came back after the 1993 Oslo Peace Accord), Rana did all she could to assimilate into this 'village-like society,' as the returnees often said. She married a rich West Bank banker, acquired a well known mother-in-law, volunteered her time in more than one cultural organisation and spoke, or more accurately imitated, local accents: a skill she acquired growing up as a child in Beirut and also by living in many other places, including Tunis. But at the end of the day she, like most returnees, knew they couldn't, and probably didn't want to, be one of '*Ahel il balad*' (the locals).

In addition to being called returnees they had many other names: 'Tunisians' in reference to Tunis where they spent some twelve years (1982-1994) after being forced out of Lebanon after the 1982 Israeli invasion; '*salata*' (salad) as opposed to *sulta* (authority), referring to their bad management; and 'Felashas', referring to Ethiopian Jewish immigrants, much discriminated against in Israel, and so it went.

Often, the story of 'returnees' and locals reminds me of Miriam who was called *al-Gharibeh* (the stranger) by all the villagers of 'Ebwein, where she lived for some sixty years. And when one day I enquired about the reason why she was called the 'stranger', she was totally surprised: "*Walao* (wow), Suad, can't you tell from my accent! I come from Jilijlieh." Her village of origin, Jilijlieh, was literally four kilometers away from 'Ebwien!

Fadia, the third newly acquired CRIME member, walked in relatively quietly. As always, beaming Fadia had a blushed face, a cynical smile with tight stretched lips, a slight movement of the head left and right, and neatly cut blond hair. With Fadia one never knows when reality ends and a joke starts. She went around greeting us one by one, and with every two kisses on the cheeks, cracked a funny line:

"Hi!" followed by a kiss and, "How did you figure out I don't have a sex life any more? Why did you waste so much time, you could have invited me at least two or three years ago." Then a beaming smile followed by a shout of laughter: ha ... ha ... ha ... ha ...

"Hi, there!" followed by two loud kisses and, "If I saw my husband in bed with a woman I would think he's giving her a biology class," another big smile followed by an even louder laugh.

"Hello!" followed by a bigger kiss and, "Get ready for tomorrow's elections. Hamas has already changed the red and yellow traffic lights to green. They've also painted all the yellow cabs green." Red was the Popular Front flag and yellow, the Initiative (*al-mubadarah*) flag, both leftist parties.

"How are you?" followed by a special kiss and, "No need for out-of-the-country medical transfers; from now on all illnesses will be treated by *sheiks* reciting the Quran." Murad, Flora's husband, was being treated in an Amman hospital. Fadia continued around the table: "Look at you ... Wow, *you* of all people should know that Saudi Arabia contributed 60,000 *dishdsheh* and *hijab*, and Oman 60,000 swords to Hamas," followed by ha, ha, ha.

I could see Rana getting all worked up: "Fine ... Hamas wants to force us into wearing the *hijab*? Let them try. They'll certainly regret it. I will design the sexiest *hijab* possible, bright green, tight, with glittering beads filling the head cover and this part," she put her hands on her bosom. "My *hijab* will make them give up the idea completely!" Like Aida with men, Rana, a typical PLO mainstream Fatah, was so irritated by Hamas she couldn't even take a joke.

100

Only after the three new CRIME members stormed in, did I understand why Majdi didn't utter a single flattering remark when he saw me and other old CRIMEs ascend the stairs to the VIP room.

Looking back at our nominations, I often wonder whether having a personal tragedy in each one's life was the subconscious criterion for selection.

8

Rana

Beirut, Winter 1978

It was the absence of my Dad, the sense of obligation towards Mum, and the unbearable halo of a Palestine on the horizon that shaped the early years of my childhood and a perpetual everlasting out-of-place consciousness.

"One, two, three, aaaand four
"One, two, three, aaaand four
"Straight legs, Maghda . . . and

"One, two, three, aaaand four,
"Look in the mirror, Nada . . . and
"One, two, three and four.
"Tohhhes, tohhhes, yes toes . . . much better, Rana . . . and
"One, two, three, aaaand four."

Concentrating fully, I was following the mirror image of Miss Maya's graceful arm movements and her beautiful slender legs as she stood on the very tips of her toes. Adamant that we all wear white or pink ballet costumes, she herself was in a tight black outfit which contrasted stunningly with her gold-blond straight hair.

"One, two, three, aaand four."

Miss Maya kept her count as she hovered around the dozen or so ballet students. Our ages, then, ranged between six and twelve; mostly girls except for Fadi and Rami. I was probably the eldest.

"One, two, three, aaand four," she intoned in her imposing voice, in the difficult task of overriding Tchaikovsky's *Swan Lake*.

My eyes were moving steadily between Miss Maya's swift movements, and those of Maghda and mine. I wanted to make sure that I was at least as good as, if not better than, my best classmate.

"Verrry good! All right now, that's it for today. We *all* need a bit more practice for next time, right Maghda?" said Ms. Maya as she looked at the unsure Maghda.

"Yes, sure, Miss Maya."

The second the music stopped, we all ran hurriedly down the freezing cold alleys of La College de Dance du Ras Beyrout. Our skinny exposed legs were turning blue. In no time, as instructed by my mother, I helped both Shirin and Suhair, my younger sisters, into their multi-layer clothing: pullovers, coats, boots, woollen scarves and hats.

Carrying bags bigger than ourselves, we ran and pushed one another down the hallway and the staircase that took us to al-Hamra Street where drivers and fathers, but mostly mothers, came to pick up their kids. Every time they came to fetch us, cars behind us, in front of us and to the side would be beeping furiously, drivers screaming and cursing. It was our twice a week ballet classes that caused a traffic jam in an already crowded street. The unbearable noise forced me to press my palms over my ears and thank God that Mum didn't know how to drive and so never had to pick us up.

The four of us, Maghda, Shirin, Suhair and myself, were looking around trying to spot Ali, Maghda's family driver. We spotted the car soon enough but not Ali, who often stood next to the black Chevrolet waving at us. As we got closer, we realised it was Tante Leila, Maghda's Mum, who had come to pick us up this afternoon.

My heart skipped a beat. I looked sideways at my sister Shirin, who knew it all. The slight smile on her lips made me realise that we were stuck, we had no other choice for a lift home this afternoon.

Maghda sat in the front seat next to her Mum, while the three of us slipped into the back seat, one after the other. I made sure my two sisters went in before me.

"*Bonsoir,* Tante!" the three of us greeted her together, like good schoolgirls.

"*Bonsoir, cheries, comment allez vous? Bien?*" replied Tante Leila in her typical Lebanese-French accent.

"Ehhh, *habibti* Maghda (yes, darling Maghda), was Miss Maya happy with your performance today?" enquired Tante Leila, this time in Arabic, in her typical strong Ras Beirut accent.

Wanting to be a theatre actress and hoping to become as famous, if not more than, the two Lebanese actors, Shosho and Nidal Ashqar, I made sure to master all accents and imitate the voices and movements of everyone around me. This was, of course, a great source of fun but, more often, as great a source of trouble. Dad especially, but later Mum and Radi, Shosho's son (who was my theatre partner at school) all encouraged my obsession.

Mastering all accents, especially the Beiruti-Lebanese and the Jerusalem-Palestinian, helped me become an *insider* whenever it was required, and an *outsider* whenever it suited me.

This gave me temporary comfort but also wore me out.

It gave me a false sense of assimilation but also made me extremely self-conscious.

It was the source of my integration but also the reason for my exclusion.

The power of accents intrigued me, and my overwhelming desire to belong to a place often made me feel completely out-of-place.

I was sulking in the back seat recalling Tante Leila's recent telephone conversation with my mother. Though Maghda and I were best friends, Tante Leila and Mum, never met or talked, except for that *one* phone conversation:

"*Bonsoir, s'il vous plait,* may I speak to Madam Taha?"

I recognised her voice instantly. Carefully placed the receiver on the table, and ran to the kitchen to get my mother.

As is often the case, I was extremely curious. I stood there watching Mum as I tried to figure out the reason for Tante Leila's out-of-the-blue phone call.

"*Masa il-Khaiiiir* (good evening)," replied Mum in her heavy Jerusalem accent. I always wondered why, after so many years in Beirut, she never altered her accent or mixed Arabic with the little French she knew from her school in Jerusalem.

I could hear Tante Leila's poignant high-pitched voice from where I stood.

"Madame, I want to tell you something. Please don't misunderstand me or get upset with me. Madame, your daughter Rana has *an extremely* wild imagination. Whenever she comes to visit my daughter Maghda, she says strange things. I mean, she is a bit weird or perhaps a bit abnormal. I don't know where she gets her stories from. She probably spends too much time in front of the television. I talked to my husband and he seems to agree with me. Madame, you have to take your daughter to a psychiatrist. I'm sorry Madame, but your daughter is a liar, a big liar."

I totally froze while Mum's face turned pale and her jaw dropped. It was not long before she interrupted Tante Leila by saying: "Madame. Madame, please, hold on a second. I have no clue what you're talking about, no idea what you're referring to. Just tell me, what is it she lied about? And believe me, I know what I must do when it comes to punishing her. Madame, I want you to know that I have dedicated my whole life to the well-being of my four daughters."

It was no longer clear to me who was more confused, Mum or Tante Leila whom I could still hear: "I don't know, Madame, she says lots of strange things. Whenever I pass by or enter Maghda's room I hear her say things like: 'I am very good at shooting, I know how to use all kinds of weapons, we wear military uniforms, smear our faces with black mud, crawl on the ground, climb up and down ropes and nets in no time, we also dig war ditches ...' and so on and so forth, Madame. She tells Maghda she learned all this in a camp somewhere up in the mountains. When Maghda once asked her if she could join, Rana replied: 'Only if your father dies. If he dies you can come with us, not only to the mountains but also to Moscow,

Berlin, Prague and many other nice places.' And when Maghda objected: 'But why should my father die first?' Rana replied: 'My friend Samira was very happy when her father died because *only then* could she come with us to Cuba!'"

"And what else does Rana talk about?" my Mum enquired as her facial expression changed from that of complete astonishment to understanding.

"Well, she says things like, these camps and trips are only for fatherless children; or what she calls *awlad o banat esh-shhada* (sons and daughters of martyrs)."

"Oh ... I see ...," replied Mum, in a matter of fact tone.

"I ultimately decided to call you, Madame, because things were getting worse by the day. You know what she told us yesterday?"

"No. No idea," replied Mum.

"Well, she said that her father was *a batal* (hero) and a *shahid* (martyr). She said that he hijacked an airplane to Tel Aviv airport. Although the Israelis shot him dead, for two years you were expecting him to come back home. And that's exactly when I decided your daughter needed therapy."

My Mum was utterly silent and in a total daze, which was always the case whenever Dad's name or stories were mentioned.

Tante Leila continued her torrent of accusations: "She also says Arafat, George Habash, Najah Wakim and many other famous personalities come to visit you at home all the time ... and ... and ..."

I could see that Mum had stopped listening and was searching for the appropriate words:

"Madame Khamis, *please*! I want to tell you something. Ali, my husband, was truly a hero and a *shahid*. Rana loves her father and she is extremely *proud* of him. She is very proud to be Palestinian ... and ... and ..."

At that moment, I had an overwhelming urge to somehow stop Mum's speech, rather than Tante Leila's.

I wanted to scream at her and say: "Stop it!"

I wanted to tell her that I was no longer either proud of my Dad or of being Palestinian as *both* have become agonising burdens.

I wondered if Mum ever realised that neither I nor my sisters ever uttered a word or a phrase that revealed we were Palestinian. We all *made sure* to leave her Jerusalem accent behind the minute we stepped over the threshold of our house into the outside world of Lebanese Beirut.

Oh, how much I wanted to be Lebanese, and so I perfected their accent.

I wanted her to know how *mad* I was at Dad; if he *really* loved us he wouldn't have walked out of the door so casually the morning he decided to disappear and hijack a plane which resulted in his death. I shall never forgive him for not even saying: "Farewell, my darlings, I shall never see you again."

But I also wanted her to know how much I *missed* him.

I wanted to tell her how happy, but also sad, I was when Maghda's father played with us, *especially with me.*

I could never tell whether he played with me out of pity or out of love.

Being *bint esh-shahid* (the daughter of a martyr), I could no longer distinguish real love from pity; not only from Maghda's father but from everyone.

I broke down, crying.

My Mum put down the receiver and came to reason with

me: "It's okay, *habibti* Rana, no one except *you and I* can ever understand how much we love Daddy and how proud of him we both are."

I was thinking that *no one*, no one, including you Mum, can ever understand how *angry* and *resentful* I have become lately of Ali, of you, and of everyone.

After his death, Mum would always include me whenever she spoke about her feelings towards her husband. When Dad was alive, she and I competed for his love. I still vividly remember how jealous I was whenever Dad picked her up and disappeared behind the closed door of their bedroom. I would bang on the door and scream at them to open it. I could hear their laughter before the long silence. Out of revenge I would wear the high-heeled red shoes and low-cut dresses which Dad brought Mum from his latest trip abroad. I would go round and round the house until they both reappeared; Dad would laugh and Mum would pretend to be mad at me.

My thoughts were interrupted by Mum's conciliatory words: "It's going to be okay, darling. Tante Leila, like many others, doesn't really know."

I didn't want her to utter one more word, as I'd heard it all before, over and over again.

All I ever wanted from her in the past, now, and once again is that warm hug; that reassuring hug that I have been seeking forever and waiting for. But since the day Ali went out to die, neither he nor she ever hugged me again.

―――――

I was awakened by her shrieking and wailing. The morning sun's rays had just hit our bedroom window. I jumped out of bed and ran to see her. She was screaming, yelling and slapping her cheeks. I was so scared, I stood still. As I came closer, she opened the door of the house and ran down the stairs. I ran behind her and held tight to her *robe de chambres*. She went to see Umm Hasan, the telephone operator and asked her for a phone line. They both looked at the newspaper my Mum held in her hand, and the yelling and weeping started all over again.

I cried, too.

Mum ran upstairs, still moaning. I followed her as she rushed into Dad's office. From his desk she picked up a small piece of paper on which he had written the name of his hotel, its phone number and his room number. She ran to the living room, picked up the phone and dialled an extremely long number. After a rather long wait a man's voice came on the other end of the line. I could hear Mum repeating Dad's first and last names: "Ali, Ali Taha, A-L-I first name, T-A-H-A family name, yes Taha," she kept repeating. "Try this number, try this name, try this date, yes, I am absolutely sure, he gave it to me."

"Sorry, Madam, there is no one here with *this* name."

Tired of repeating it, the hotel receptionist hung up on her. Mum tried again and again until she collapsed totally.

The crying and screaming resumed.

Not realising what was it all about I did exactly the same.

For hours on end our phone kept ringing. With every new call Mum repeated exactly the same conversation but with another new sob. The loudest cry was when 'anti Suhaylah, my father's eldest sister, called from Amman.

"Come with me," said Tante Samira, as she took me with her, my three sisters tagging along. Up the stairs we went to

110

her apartment one floor above. She got us to wash our faces, brush our teeth, and tried to feed us. To no avail. As we descended the stairs on our way to the school bus downstairs, many men and wailing women came running in the opposite direction.

All in black.

Shirin, Suhair and I got on to the school auto-car. By then I realised that something terrible had happened. Not knowing exactly what it was, I hugged both sisters very tightly.

It was not long before we separated—I to first grade upstairs, and they to toddlers downstairs.

I purposely went to Ahmad, the school guard, and asked: "Can I take the newspaper up to the headmaster?"

"Oh, thanks ... that's very sweet of you," he said as he handed it to me.

I carried it with me and half-way up the stairs, I stopped and stared at the front page—there was Dad's photograph spread out across it. I tried to read what was written underneath, but with my difficult first grade reading ability I spelled out: *sha-hii-d*, yes, *shahid*. I had no clue what *shahid* meant. I folded the paper up again and went straight to the headmaster's office.

"Good morning, Rana. How are you today, sweetie?" he asked in a friendly tone, one I never heard him use with other students. I was the daughter of his very best friend, Ali.

"Ammo Adnan (Uncle Adnan) what is the meaning of *shahid*?" I posed the question, hiding the newspaper behind my back.

"Sweetie, *shahid* is the one who dies for his country; he loves his country so much that he is ready to die for it."

"Does it mean that Dad loves his country Palestine more than he loves us? Or does it mean that Daddy is dead?" I asked as I handed him the newspaper.

He was crying like a baby.

I left him and walked towards my classroom. Ms. Siham was standing in front of the class, and as I walked in she enquired: "And why are we late today?"

"Ms. Siham, what does it mean to die?" I asked immediately.

"Isn't it a bit early for such questions, Rana? Why don't you sit on your bench and get your books out of your bag?"

"Daddy died ... he is also a *shahid*." I tried it the other way round, "Daddy is a *shahid* and he died." I continued testing the reactions to these two bizarre words that day, until I was sent home.

My mother was sitting there motionless, colourless and emotionless. Her glassy eyes scared me. Recalling Ms. Siham's morning descriptions I thought Mum had also died. From a distance I watched apprehensively as two women in black approached her. They stood right next to her and held her hands. As they tried to remove the red nail polish on her fingers, Mum started yelling and screaming her head off—she was pushing and pulling as her, "No-o-o-o-o-o!" filled the skies. I put my palms to my ears and closed my eyes. When I opened them again, Mum had resigned herself to their will.

With Mum's red nail polish gone, I realised that something truly terrible had taken place.

I was watching it all from a distance. I wanted to come near her but was much too scared. Scared of the women in black around her and of all the strangers in our house. I looked at Mum and she was different. Very different. No longer the Mum

I had always had. Some unseen barrier came up between us, a barrier that separated me from her. I wanted to run to her, hold her tight and tell her, "Mum, I am here."

I didn't have the courage to do it and she wasn't there to notice it.

The distance that separated us that day remained between us forever.

I stood at one end of the room, scared, and she was not there at the other end of that same room.

Little did I realise then that this distance and barrier would be life-long, it would outlive both of our strong wills.

Coming of Age

Beirut, 1979

I was consciously and slowly breaking away from my mother's designated role and our lives as the martyr Ali's wife and daughters.

Soon after Dad's death, my three sisters and I acquired many 'privileges', mostly from Dad's PLO friends and particularly from its Chairman, Yasser Arafat. This resulted in our transfer from the modest Palestinian refugee camp school of Ammo Adnan to that of the elitist Ras Beirut school. Except for me, my sisters, and a few others, most of the school's students and teachers were Lebanese.

Once again, the school's headmaster, Ammo Taisir, was one of my father's closest friends. He was also Palestinian. Unlike my first headmaster, Ammo Adnan, I made sure I referred to the new headmaster as *ustaz* (Sir). However, that did not stop

Ustaz Taisir from reminding me, at the end of *every* semester, of my *expected duty* (as the daughter of his late friend) to excel in all my studies.

My adolescent world in school, but more importantly out of school, was being shaped around my Lebanese classmates and their many exciting activities. Everything was allowed, provided we had completed our homework for the day, as well as the extra-curricular activities which ranged from piano to ballet classes, theatre to modern dance. As was the case with me, but also with many others, our extra-curricular activities tended to fulfil our mothers' aspirations and desires rather than our own. As teenage schemers, extra-curricular activities gave us the necessary excuse to sneak away, every now and then, with our sweethearts to hamburger joints and ice cream parlours, which soon turned into sunset strolls along the Corniche il-Rauche and, later, to wild weekend parties.

As time passed—except for my mountain martyrs' children's summer training camps and trips abroad—I was spending almost all my time with my Lebanese classmates, Nada and Fadi, but primarily with my favourite girlfriend, Maghda. Iyad, also a Lebanese schoolmate whom I have known for years now was, like his mother, Tante Fadia, a solid bridge connecting my two different worlds and my schizophrenic life: the sadness and heaviness of virtual *homeland* Palestine, and the fun and excitement of *hometown* Beirut—at war with itself but also with us Palestinians.

For years, most of Mum's friends and ours were the wives and children of martyrs. As was often the case, one afternoon they had all gathered in our house. Tante Fadia, whom we loved dearly, was accompanied this time by Iyad, her dashingly beautiful son.

While Mum's friends sat in the salon, being the eldest, I was instructed to take all the children into our living room inside to play. The minute Iyad stepped into our house, l developed an instant crush on him; he was tall and slim, with big black eyes and long wavy blond hair. My instinctive reaction was to grab his attention immediately. I looked at him and, as loudly and demonstratively as possible, I asked him:

"*Iyaaad*, is your father dead or alive?"

Iyad's rosy cheeks blushed. He was totally at a loss. He looked me and at the other children around him and said: "What? I don't quite understand."

"We *all* want to know whether your father is a *shahid* or is still alive?" I insisted.

"Dad is alive, of course," Iyad replied. I sensed his pride.

"Sorry, Iyad, you can't play with us, we *only* play with martyrs' children," I said in a commander's voice.

Iyad ran out seeking his mother's help. It was not long before he returned with *my* Mum, who was holding his hand.

"Rana . . . *habibti,* what you just said to Iyad is not very *kind.* You can't exclude him just because his father is still alive."

"Well, Mum, instead of intervening on his behalf why don't you pray that his father becomes a *shahid* very soon?"

Smiling nervously, Mum disappeared, and Iyad had a beaming victorious grin on his gorgeous face.

Not only did Iyad succeed in playing with me that afternoon, he also managed to seduce me for many years to come. Or was it the other way around?

As always, I had to take the initiative of inviting Iyad out. He was shy and I was outgoing. Perhaps it was his shyness that made my mother comfortable about her daughter's crush. The very careful choice of my tight outfit revealed it all, and he being the son of her best friend also helped.

"Mum, Iyad and I would like to go out, have a bite and then go and see a film this afternoon."

"Fine, *but* don't be late."

I always formulated my requests as statements, and she always affirmed her authority with a 'but'.

I was in seventh heaven; walking along the buzzing chic al-Hamra Street, passing by elegant shops, cafés and restaurants in the company of the most beautiful boy in town. I was proud and confident. This made my already animated way of walking, talking, pointing, joking and imitating people's accents and movements even more expansive.

Iyad, who looked absolutely gorgeous in his white jeans and soft blue shirt, was tentatively listening, laughing and responding to me in his own subtle and delicate way.

Wanting to be on time for the movie he calmly finished eating his hamburger while I, because of my non-stop chattering, had to quickly swallow mine as we stood up to leave.

Not knowing what films were showing in the many cinemas around us, and not really caring which one we saw as long as we sat next to each other in the semi-darkness of the movie theatre, I suggested we see the film highly recommended by Tante Fadia.

"You must go and see this film, it is just wonderful, really wonderful. I haven't seen such a good film in so long."

Being a gentleman, Iyad went to get the tickets, I went to buy the biggest popcorn paper cup, lots of chocolates, chips and candy. I wanted to make sure that the exchange of snacks would last the full ninety minutes of the film.

I was getting more and more apprehensive as I realised that *this* was really our first date. Though Iyad and I had been to the movies alone and with friends many times before, it somehow felt *very* different this time. We were both acting a bit nervous and funny. The excitement of it all accentuated our intrinsic characters—I, bubbling, he, sober and quiet.

I was looking around hoping not to see any of my classmates, friends, or for that matter anyone at all that I knew. I had planned to find secluded seats at the very end on a side aisle row. To my utter surprise the theatre was completely packed. We looked around and finally spotted two seats in the very first row. Being more self-conscious than ever, I felt as if everyone was whispering and staring at me and my good-looking boyfriend. Wow! Attractive me, handsome Iyad, I didn't realise till that moment that we would soon become the talk of the town as the cute *couple*.

The minute the film started, we sank into our seats and leaned towards each other. I was trying to free my right hand in anticipation of his move, or if it came to that, mine. It wasn't long before we were both totally immersed in the unbelievable scenes of this out-of-this-world film. It was extremely strange and weird, but also wonderful. We sat up straight and shrank into the middle of our seats. I was getting all worked up, sweating all over, torn between two overwhelming feelings— being well behaved and suggesting we leave, or being true to myself, curious to see all. As the film progressed, I was getting more and more embarrassed, my head lowered while my eyes were fixed on the screen.

The ninety-minute film felt longer than my fourteen-year life. When the film ended, we were both sunk in our seats, totally flabbergasted, waiting for the crowds to disappear. Only then did I realise that it was not us, but the wild beauty and actions of Marlon Brando that were the talk of the town.

In no time at all, I acquired Iyad's characteristics—quiet, shy and, for once, speechless. I slowly ascended the two flights of stairs taking me up to our house.

The minute I uttered the four (scandalous) words: *Last Tango in Paris*, I received a stinging slap on the face. I argued in vain; it was *her* friend, not mine, who had recommended the film.

And for months to come, it was the ninety minutes with Marlon Brando, not Iyad, that were the source of my fantasies.

9

Maya

It was ten minutes past four. I woke up before the break of dawn, just in time to shut the alarm. I had stuck it under my pillow so as not to wake my younger brother, Omar. His bed was right next to mine. Mum and Dad's bedroom was on the other side of the house so there was no fear that they would hear me leave at this hour.

It was the summer vacation. If caught, I couldn't have claimed I was on my way to school. Mum always said: "The worst thing in life is to lie ... only cowards lie." I was certainly not a coward, I was a "born leader," as Mum frequently said. Leaders shouldn't lie, and shouldn't let their comrades down. That's why I couldn't sleep all night.

I had decided not to include Omar in our mission. Being three years younger than me, I didn't think this difficult task was suitable for a seven-year old boy. In all our neighbourhood wrestling, Omar always cried and was afraid. He lacked the necessary courage for this task. I also thought it would be

119

nice if Mum and Dad were left with at least one child, just in case I got lost or never came back.

We were five: Razan, my best girlfriend from school, Iyad, Majdi and his brother, Ramzi—the three strongest boys in the neighbourhood. Since I was the head of the cell (*khaliyyeh*), I gave the orders and they obeyed. From scouts' trips I learned that we must pack lots of water, tons of canned food, many chocolates and energy bars. Before I went to bed the night before, I sneaked into our kitchen and just in case, made two sandwiches each: jam for energy and thyme for memory. I instructed everyone to meet in Dad's garage at five a.m. sharp: "Not a minute earlier and not a minute later." I also made sure they all knew how to read the maps which I had drawn accurately days in advance. So as to get life-long comradeship, I made them swear: "We promise not to reveal our plot, not to get scared, not to change our minds, and if caught by the army, not to ever confess." We were all set. Hearts pumping, we parted.

The same day I accompanied Mum to the big prison in Nablus where Uncle Khalid and Uncle Baha were to remain for seven years. Uncle Khalid was Mum's youngest brother, and Uncle Baha was Majdi's and Ramzi's eldest brother. They were in the same class, the same cell, and were arrested by Israeli soldiers on the same night. A day after they were arrested the army arrived, ordered Grandpa and Grandma out of the house, put up barbed wire around the area, and dynamite inside the house. Mum cried when she saw the bulldozer approach her house. The neighbours said: "The army is getting ready to blow up the house." I thought of all the nice furniture inside and I also cried, because I loved

Grandpa's big new house. I wondered where we would go now for Friday's festive lunches with all my uncles, aunts and many, many cousins. But in the end, Grandpa's phone calls and meetings with lawyers, friends and important politicians stopped the army from demolishing his house.

Like Mum, I loved Uncle Khalid the most. He brought me lots of sweets, sat me on his lap, read me nice books and the poetry he and Grandpa loved. He giggled often and told me funny stories that made me laugh. But in prison I was shaky and scared. Mum had warned me that children my age never visit prisons. But I insisted so much that she finally gave in. The minute I saw the soldiers, I clutched her tightly. I didn't know what had happened to Uncle who was always well dressed. In prison he, like the others, wore dirty white and blue pajamas. He was unshaven and his eyes were puffy. When Mum asked him how he was, he replied: "In great spirits, but I haven't slept much as the interrogations went on day and night." Ten minutes later, the terrible soldiers said our time was up. All mothers, sisters and daughters cried as they said goodbye. On the way back home, I asked Mum what interrogation was, but she didn't reply. She just cried and cried and cried.

In the silence of the darkness I took off my pajamas, put on my olive green training suit and my new walking shoes. I threw my heavy rucksack on my back, and made sure not to leave behind the maps which I had placed in the big pocket of my rucksack. I opened the door carefully, snuck out, and shut it behind me. I celebrated the success of this crucial first step, took a deep breath, and on tiptoe, ran down the two flights of stairs which took me to Dad's garage. I looked at my watch, it was five a.m. I stuck my head out of the garage door and there they were. One was late. Since, as agreed, we had all covered our heads with black and white *kuffiyyeh*, I didn't know who it was who hadn't arrived. But from their voices I could tell that the missing person was my girlfriend, Razan. Not wanting them to think that girls were cowards, I gave the order: "We wait for exactly five minutes, then leave." As we waited anxiously for her, to my utter shock, Omar appeared. He argued and argued and then begged to join us, but I refused. I ordered him to go back home and warned him not to utter a single word. As was often the case, he cried. I gave my command to proceed and off we went. Just before we disappeared into the narrow and crooked alleys of Nablus' old town, I looked back—Omar was still there. We took a left turn and walked in the direction of the big mountains behind which lay Lebanon. A few hastily marched steps, and I could hear Mum's frantic yells. I dropped the maps and froze. By the time Mum dragged me home by the ear, the others had disappeared.

Like Uncle Khalid, I was interrogated for hours and hours, and was also not allowed to sleep until I finally confessed: "We were on our way to the south of Lebanon to join the *fidaeen* (freedom fighters) in their military training, come back well equipped, attack the prison and free Uncle Khalid and Uncle Baha." Though it was her brother whom I wanted to set free, I lost my own freedom for a whole week: no more playing Israeli Army and Palestinian Freedom Fighters in the empty building behind, no more bicycle acrobatics in the streets, and no more joining the boys in our neighbourhood fights. What worried me most was that, with no further training, I would no longer be the goalkeeper for our football team. Being a girl, many boys competed for this post. It also gave our neighbours' two nasty girls yet another chance to mock me: "You're barefoot like a gypsy, in pants like a tomboy (*hasan sabi*)." This really got me. Since I was sure I was a girl, it made me cry. I put on my sandals—which I had taken off to play in the streets—and ran back home. Mum was totally surprised as this was the first time ever that I, not Omar, had come home crying. With her encouragement I went to my bedroom, opened my cupboard and brought down the new clothes Mum and Dad had brought back from Cairo. They were still in the paper wrapping. I put on the brown leather skirt, the brick-coloured blouse, and the striped brown and brick stockings that matched the outfit. In addition I wore my ladylike brown shoes, and had Mum help me comb my hair. I went out of the door and to my utter delight, the girls were still there. I walked up and down the street showing off my elegant costume. Once they left, pretending not to care, I ran home, back to my training suit, and was off barefoot to the football match with the rest of the boys.

Mum was truly troubled by my Lebanon plot, but kept repeating the story to all our family members and friends with a smile. This I did not understand. She also told Uncle Khalid and Uncle Baha, who she reported, laughed out loud, then almost cried. After her next visit to the prison Uncle Khalid sent me a small stone on which he had inscribed: "*Faleestin lana,*" Palestine is Ours. I knew Uncle Khalid was proud of me. And so was Mum.

I forgot to say, from that day on, Omar's nickname became 'collaborator' (*ed-dasoos*), till the day the Israeli soldiers shot a spray of bullets into his tummy. He crawled bleeding, until some people rushed him to the hospital, pleading that the boy was dying. No one knew who he was until the doctor in residence arrived: "Oh, my God, it is my boy!" Omar was saved by a good surgeon's trembling hands, but that was six years later, when he was thirteen.

It wasn't long before I went back to my tomboyish life. But as time went by, like Mum, I did more and more voluntary work. With other teenage boys and girls, we cleaned up the streets, visited refugee camps, joined reading circles, had guitar and dancing lessons, and took part in most demonstrations. When Mum wasn't around, I also joined in in throwing stones at military jeeps, until one day I was chased and caught. The Israeli soldiers placed me on the hood of the jeep and went around town. Horrified, I started crying. The speed with which the news reached Mum was faster than that of the jeep itself. Once more she came screaming and yelling, this time at the soldiers, and after much pushing and pulling they eventually let go of me.

Coming of Age

Mum's Notebook and Reception Istiqbal, 1979

It was a last-minute inspection. Mum stood next to the dining table with her TC-WW notebook *(Ja'oo wa thabna)*, or what Omar later referred to as the earliest version of GIS (geographic information system). Mum had taken one of Dad's thick patients' record notebooks to which she had added many columns. On top of each she scribbled a letter or two: when Omar and I got curious, she explained:

"TC stands for They Came, WW stands for We Went, PTB for Presents They Brought, PWT for Presents We Took, and the two letters on top of each column stand for the first and family names of my friends. A number combined with a letter means the day of the reception—for example, 1M is the first Monday of the month, 3T stands for the third Tuesday of the month, and so on. And here is the menu served at each woman's reception, and ..."

At this point I was at a total loss. There was a list of some thirty names. In addition, like my Lebanon maps, Mum's had sketches of the town's different neighbourhoods illustrating the location of her friend's house and her telephone numbers. Mum's notebook was untidy like her, but it had lots of details and valuable information. I was truly amazed, but also a bit surprised by her ability to keep a register of the exceptionally complicated women's receptions *(istiqbalat)* in a big town like Nablus. I guess Mum was caught between her activist nature, the web-like social obligations of her own family's prestigious standing, and Dad's status as a self-made man *(isami)*. But what impressed me most was her ability to manage it all: she took very good care of me and of Omar. She took care of Dad, of her parents, her friends and the neighbours, in addition to volunteering much of her time to charitable organisations. But *this* record topped them all.

Mum and Dad fell in love when they were teenagers. Her father was a big shot in town, while her beloved came from a simple peasant background. Mum's eldest brother, Ahmad, threatened to kill Dad if he didn't stop loving her. Though Mum was beautifully irresistible, Dad was truly scared. Like everyone else he knew the story of Grandpa getting away with killing a striking schoolteacher. Grandpa was then the headmaster and the dead teacher, like Dad, came from a village nearby. But Mum was adamant, and Grandpa loved her and didn't want her to remain a spinster.

————

I was helping Mum put the finishing touches to her reception preparations: the tens of lined-up hubble-bubbles, huge cigarette plates, fresh orange and lemon juice already set in trays, another tray with coffee and tea cups, and the expanded dining table with at least twenty varieties of eats: pastries, *tabouleh*, small pizzas, all sorts of meat pies, cakes, cookies, Jell-O, ice cream and assorted Arabic sweets, in addition to the typical Nablus sweet, *knafeh*, which she had ordered from the very best sweet-shop in town.

While Mum was lining up the four musical instruments: the *oud*, the wooden flute, the drum, and the *daf*, I heard her say: "Please, darling, this time you *must* dance. I know you don't like dancing at women's receptions, but it is not *proper* to have *their* daughters dance while you just stand there."

Mum knew I loved dancing so much that, years later, I became a modern dancer. But this was different. She never asked me, and I never accompanied her to her Nablus women's receptions. I was determined not to be part of the fashion and beauty contests where young women danced while mothers chose a pretty bride for their sons, brothers or male cousins. Neither Mum nor I wanted to marry that way or that early. Even if I did, I stood little chance in a place where being white, blond, with blue or green eyes and tiny features was all they cared for. Caught in the middle of it all, and having personally suffocated from the town's social obligations, Mum never pushed me. For her sake, I quietly dressed up as stylishly as the rest of the teenage girls and self-consciously stood next to her while she received her guests, whose heavy perfumes announced their arrival way in advance:

"Hi, darling … how are you, Maya? Look at you, this is the first time I've see you in a dress, it suits you better than the boyish clothes you always wear."

In less than a minute another of Mum's friends arrived, accompanied by her two teenage daughters almost my age:

"Hi, Maya *habibti* … How are you (*keefek*)? How is school?" She looks at Mum and continues: "Though dark, your daughter is cute."

"Hi, Maya, *keefek, habibti*? You're still very skinny, you'd better eat, otherwise who's going to marry a skeleton?" She gave me two big kisses on the cheeks.

"Hi, *habibti, keefek*? How is school?" I was delighted there was no other comment. A minute later I heard her tell Mum, "Haya … If you want your *only* daughter to get married, it's high time you took her to Beirut or even Amman for a nose job … otherwise, she is okay."

I stood there welcoming more of Mum's guests:

"Hi, Maya *habibti, keefek*? How is school? You know there are green contact lenses nowadays. This way you can get rid of your heavy glasses, and your black eyes become green and beautiful." Moa … Moa, more kisses on my cheeks.

"Hi, Maya *habibti, keefek* … how is school? I like your long wavy hair but now that you're a young woman, it will look even better if Mum allowed you to dye it reddish-brown. This way your dark complexion will also look lighter."

Once the women were done giving me, the other daughters, but also one another 'compliments', it was time to go round distributing; hubble-bubbles to the older women and cigarettes to the more fashionable ones. I carried the first hubble-bubble and gave it to Aunt Leila: "Is this real tobacco or honeyed apple tobacco?"

"Real tobacco," I replied.

"No, *habibti,* this is too heavy for me. Can I have honeyed apple?"

I went back to the kitchen and brought two honeyed apples. I handed her one and the other to the woman sitting right next to her:

"Is this real tobacco or honeyed apple?" asked the second woman. "Honeyed apple," I replied.

"No, *habibti,* this is too light for me. Can I have real tobacco?"

I don't know why each one seemed to want the opposite of what I offered. As I went in and out I overheard two women arguing about the colour of our new curtains. As I got closer one of them pulled me by the hand and asked: "Are your curtains dirty or are they this colour?"

Not knowing what to make of her nasty comment, I said: "Let me ask Mum."

"No, no *habibti* ... really no need." I purposely walked towards Mum but said nothing. When it was time to pass the juice trays, all the girls rushed to help. Juice rounds declared the beginning of the Beauty and Fashion Show. I sat on a chair and watched the many keen participants: it didn't take much to notice that it was the teenage girls who attracted the mothers and aunts who happened to have handsome potential grooms.

Half an hour or so of showing off, acting feminine and charming, and it was time to serve the food. Mum went around inviting everyone to come forward. But it is part of the tradition to take your time and pretend not to hear because it's considered rather vulgar to rush and eat. It is also part of the etiquette to go round and invite women by age and by status. But that was easy in a society like Nablus where social status, unlike age, is easily acknowledged. The pretence of not caring about food ended the minute they reached the dining table; if I weren't a witness to it all, I would have thought it was a swarm of locusts that visited us that afternoon. However, remarks about the vanished food lasted much longer than the food itself: "This needed more salt", "that needed more sugar", "this needed more oil", "that needed more baking", "this was yummy, but no ..." and so it went.

With full stomachs, the women sat back in their chairs waiting for the real entertainment: it was time for music and the belly dance. All of us 'potential brides' would take turns and dance. Mum went around distributing musical instruments: the *oud* to Tante Lamia, a well known *oud* player with a beautiful voice, the wooden flute to an older woman, the *daf* to her best friend, Hanan, and the drum to our next door neighbour, Umm Ramzi. In no time we had a quartet and in even less time, music began and the dancing followed. All the 'brides' were sitting next to each other. It was Mum who pulled teenage Salma by the hand and dragged her to the middle of the room to the dance floor, and everyone begged her to dance. Once more, the shy and not-wanting-to-dance girl turned in a flash into a seductive belly-dancer. As women clapped and sang to the music, Salma's Mum took off her elegant scarf and tied it around Salma's lower waist, accentuating her daughter's belly movements. A five-minute dance, then Salma stopped and pulled her friend, Ghada, into the middle of the dance floor. Then it was Samira's turn, after that Yara's, then Huda's and so it went, my turn totally forgotten. While the bride-selection dancing took half an hour or so, the older women's dance lasted at least three times as long. When it was time for the coffee finale, each teenage girl served her 'potential in-laws', while Mum and I served the rest.

A week or two later Salma, Samira, Ghada and Huda were formally engaged.

They flew to their golden nests, while I landed in America for my engineering degree.

Haya, July 2002

As Ayman and I checked into the hotel I looked at the clock placed right above the receptionist's desk. It was 6:10 in the evening. The two-day long World Bank conference had wiped me out.

I slid open the heavy French windows of our bedroom and stepped out onto the terrace.

I was mesmerised by the light pink and purple reflections of the Jerusalem mountains on the Dead Sea's still surface. It was truly heavenly, out of this world—and out of Palestine.

I'm always amazed by how beautiful Palestine looks from a distance, and how comforting it is to be on the opposite side: the Jordanian eastern shores of the Dead Sea.

"Ayman, why don't we stay an extra day or two? Your work and mine can wait," I said.

There was no reply. He probably didn't hear.

While my vacations start with a jacuzzi, Ayman's begin with switching on the television.

I stepped back into the room, started unpacking my huge vanity bag: facial creams, body lotions, make-up and the rest of it. Soon the beautiful yellow marble was crammed. There is something that I love about hotel bathrooms. I've often wondered why I never managed to have one at home.

I took out the novel which I had started weeks ago, and dropped into a mound of bubbles. The water was a bit hot. I adjusted myself by using my feet as brakes, pressed them against the bottom of the tub and started reading. Couldn't concentrate. Partly because I was still unwinding, partly because of the dentist's-clinic-music coming out of the loudspeakers, and partly because of Ayman's noisy television and mobile which rang a number of times.

I placed my book on the floor and decided to just *relax*. Closed my eyes. Felt the hot water warming my body. Forced myself to stop thinking about the loads of office work I had left behind. Concentrated on each of my stiff muscles: I went through them one by one and begged them to relax: toes, feet, calves, thighs, big bud, stomach, big boobs, arms, hands, fingers, shoulders, forehead, eyebrows, cheeks with wrinkles, even lips. I took two deep breaths and slipped once or twice before I stood up. I reached for the white bathrobe from behind the door and checked my wrinkles in the mirror—my face already looked relaxed.

Suddenly I noticed that there was utter silence.

Wow. How very unlike Ayman—he had switched off the television and the hotel's terrible music.

I threw myself on the huge bed and sighed: "Splendid. Ayman, the bath is all yours."

Ayman who was sitting at the edge of the blue armchair, next to the television, didn't reply. He was holding his head between his hands. His face was almost green.

I sat up straight in bed and asked: "Ayman what is it? Have I said anything wrong?"

"No, nothing … I just have a terrible stomach ache." He picked up his cigarettes and stepped out onto the terrace. I wanted to join him but decided it was better to leave him alone. I reached for the remote control and switched on the T.V. It didn't work.

"Ayman, what's wrong with the television?" I screamed out at him.

He stepped back into the room instantly and said: "The television just broke down. And the telephone doesn't work. I'll have to go and complain."

"Goddammit, we pay all this money and there is no T.V. and no phone!"

"Why don't you get dressed, let's go and eat at the Chinese restaurant downstairs."

I tried charming him but didn't succeed.

Like 'lovers' we went down hand-in-hand. He, in his white silk suit and I in a white and pink dress. "What a match," I laughed. He didn't join in.

You're probably wondering what became of the tomboyish girl you knew long ago! Well, in almost two and a half decades a lot had happened: many romances, a nose job in America, twenty more kilos, some botox and silicone injections here and there, a first marriage, a teenage daughter called Zena, and a second marriage and two daughters: Maha and Zaha, seven and five. I had become the head of the construction department in an international agency; in other words, I was fated to dress like a lady even if I didn't act like one. Not to mention pressures from Jerusalem and Nablus upper middle class in-laws, not one, but two.

I was checking the menu when restless Ayman suddenly stood up and rushed out. In the distance I could see Sirin and Raed, her fiancé. Ayman placed his arm around Sirin's shoulders and kept talking to her for quite some time.

A bit astonished to see them, I stood up and said: "What a lovely surprise! Sirin, how come you didn't tell me earlier that you were coming to the Dead Sea?" Sirin and I had been at the same conference in Amman just a few hours earlier.

"Well, we thought we'd join you for an *argieleh* (hubble-bubble). We've already eaten."

I was busy asking the waiter to set the table for four when Ayman excused himself: "I won't be long," he said as he walked a few steps then turned back: "Sirin, can I use your Jordanian mobile? I need to call a friend." She handed him her phone and he walked away.

"I don't know what it is, guys, but he's got a bad stomach and is in quite a state."

Sirin and I talked and talked, but no words or topics seemed to flow naturally. As we stood up to leave, I noticed Ayman's plate was untouched.

It was past midnight when Sirin and Raed drove back to Amman. Ayman and I walked back to our hotel room through the lush gardens, arms around each other.

"I can never figure out this Sirin, she's so moody; warm and attentive sometimes, and cold like a fish at others."

We made love that night.

Daylight was hardly breaking when I felt Ayman's tender touch on my shoulders.

"Maya ... Wake up, my darling."

"For God's sake, Ayman, what is it? We went to bed after midnight ... what time is it now?" I looked at my watch, it was quarter to five in the morning.

"We can't stay here any longer, we urgently need to go back."

He got out of bed, came around, and sat on my side. I jumped up and shouted: "What is it, Ayman? You've been acting funny ever since we arrived. Tell me what's going on."

"Listen, darling, something dreadful has happened."

Alarmed, I sank to my knees and asked, "Is it my grandma?"

"No, no."

"For God's sake, Ayman, is it the girls? Omar?"

"No, no, the girls are okay. It is partly Omar."

"Oh, MY GOD ... What do you mean *partly*?"

"No, *habibti*, it is Haya, it's your Mum," Ayman broke down, weeping.

"What? Mum? Did you say Mum? I just talked to her yesterday. Did she have a heart attack?"

"No. She was shot dead by the Israeli army yesterday at six-thirty in the evening. Your brother Omar and your Dad were also injured but they're okay now."

134

"*Ayman ... Haya was shot dead yesterday ... and you didn't tell me!*"

"Maya, *habibti,* calm down. You know very well that the Allenby Bridge closes at one in the afternoon. What would I have done with you all night if you knew? My brother Ibrahim called while you were in the shower ... and Al-Jazeera reported it ... and I purposely unplugged everything ... and ..."

I couldn't comprehend what Ayman was saying any more. I first went blank.

Then, crazy.

"God damn ... You big liar, you don't know what you're talking about. Liar ... liar ... that is a very ... bad joke ..." I opened the terrace door. Tried to push myself over the parapet. Ayman was right there. I collapsed on the terrace floor.

"I know, *habibti,* it's horrifying, it's absolutely unbelievable. Calm down now, we need to pack our things and leave." Ayman knew exactly what Mum meant to me, me in particular. I opened the door and went down the corridor to the reception hall in my nightgown. Ayman caught hold of me and helped me dress.

We were on our way to the Allenby Bridge.

For some time I kept quiet. Then kept repeating: "It's a lie ... it's a big lie ... it's a joke ... a bad joke ... No, it's not possible ... Not my Mum ... Not Haya."

It took a tragedy like my mother being killed to realise the absurdity of Israeli 'security logistics' at the Bridge. What would I tell the Israeli soldiers? We are in a hurry because you shot my mother dead in Nablus? Or: We are in a hurry because my Mum was killed in Nablus? Or: We have an emergency, can you help us through the Bridge quickly? And then they would want to know what the emergency was.

Before I got out of the bus whose passengers were curious about my condition, Ayman held me tight, looked me in the eyes and whispered: "Okay, Maya, listen to me carefully now … there are two ways of going through this: one is to scream at the motherfuckers; tell the criminals they've shot your Mum; injured your brother and your Dad; fuck the Occupation and the rest of it … But you have to understand this will get us into trouble. We'll be delayed for hours and will never get to Nablus today. Or you can keep quiet and I'll do all the talking. Please, Maya, *habibti,* let me handle this, only this one time," Ayman begged.

I stood quietly in line at twelve stations.

At one station, we handed over our bags.

At another, we went through a 'normal' security machine.

At a third, we went through an 'abnormal' or 'weird' security machine which sprinkles you, then says a few incomprehensible words.

At a fourth, we stood in one of the many long and slow passport control queues.

Then in another, to check if your passport had been checked.

Then we stood in the same queue three or four more times checking, re-checking and re-re-checking if our bags had arrived in the luggage hall.

Then like everybody else, we were randomly selected for a bag search, so we stepped aside into the luggage-search room.

Then our bags went through another security machine.

Finally we were 'allowed' into the luggage hall where we picked up our bags.

Then through Customs.

And finally we were stopped by a security woman who made sure that our bags were ours.

At two of the stations, I sat on a bench for a long, long time. I was staring at the soldiers and security officers trying to see what soldiers who kill look like. *They* were chatting and joking as if nothing had happened. Business as usual: screaming at and insulting Palestinian passengers, ordering us to stand in line, go back, come this way, go that way. All in their funny Arabic and their unbearable accents. I was thinking of Mum who adored Arabic literature, and often made us roll about laughing as she imitated them.

I burst out crying.

The second we stepped out of the building, I was in the arms of my two best friends: Arwa and Fatimeh. The minute we settled in the car, I begged them for all the details.

With a big sigh Fatimeh began: "The curfew was imposed once again on Nablus yesterday. Your Mum had placed her chair in front of the house on one of the steps of the glazed veranda."

"That's where she always fed my girls," I interrupted.

Fatimeh continued: "Your Dad was sitting on the stone parapet just next to her. She was embroidering while he plucked the thyme. It was past six in the evening when Omar opened the veranda door and started screaming and yelling at the two soldiers who were standing next to their jeep. One was pointing his rifle right at them. Before Omar knew it, there was a spray of bullets that shattered the glass of the veranda. Omar fell to the ground and screamed for help:

'Dad, I'm dying … I'm dying … one bullet went through my head.'

"Arm bleeding, your Dad turned around and knelt on the floor next to Omar. He looked at his son's injuries and said: 'Thank God the bullet didn't penetrate your head.' He stood up and looked at your Mum: she was still on the chair with a shattered head and a flood of blood: on her, on the chair, on the steps where she sat. It was the bullets, Omar's screaming and your Dad's weeping that brought the neighbours, the ambulance, and later on, half the town out. Everyone came in spite of the curfew. Head bleeding, Omar ran after the soldiers who meanwhile had got into their jeep, drove to the end of the road and came back. Looked at the crime scene and drove away. Omar ran after them yelling: 'You bastards . . . You criminals … You've killed my mother!'

"The neighbours got hold of him and pushed him into a second ambulance that had just arrived. Haya was taken to hospital in the first ambulance.

"Forty minutes of weeping and pleading got us to the Howwarah checkpoint. After many arguments, shouting and screaming we were told by the soldiers that there was no access to Nablus as the town was still under curfew. We drove around and got to Beit Eba checkpoint where the soldiers simply waved us in."

The minute I spotted the Palestinian flag, hundreds of parked cars and the wide open gate of our garden, I knew there were no ifs or buts about it: the nightmare was true.

From a distance, I glimpsed Dad behind the veranda's

shuttered glass door. Placed my foot on the first step and saw Mum's blood on the floor. At that point I screamed: "Ayman, please don't let me faint ..."

I hugged Dad. And as he wept, I heard him say: "Yes, she died ... she died ... yes, darling, she died."

"Please, Dad, tell me the truth."

"Yes, daughter ... sweet Haya died. The fuckers killed her. The *stupid* doctor stood there and couldn't do a thing. She died with me standing helplessly right next to her ... I tried, believe me, daughter, I tried but she was gone."

"Dad, tell me she will come back."

"No, darling, she won't."

At that moment I spotted Omar with a bandaged head.

He hugged me tight and spoke no words.

I let go of Omar and Dad, and walked through the many faceless people who had filled our house. Mum's poster, which had been printed that day, covered the walls. The legend under her photo read:

Haya the martyr (al-Shahideh Haya).

"Is that what's become of Mum? A poster ... a nice poster ... a *poster!*" I screamed at the top of my voice.

Someone hugged me, someone else kissed me, some formally shook my hand, some said comforting words, and others repeated mechanically:

"Be strong; your Mum is lucky; she is a *shahideh*, will go straight to heaven, what she got we all wish for ..." As the mindless bravado comments went on and on, I lost my cool. "May I ask you all to *shut up!* Whoever wants their Mum, their Dad, their brother or their daughter to be a martyr, please come forward ... raise your hand ... I don't want my

139

Mum to be a *shahideh* and I don't want her to be a poster," I wept uncontrollably.

A few days later, I learnt that the owner of the print shop and many young activists (*esh-shabab*) wanted to cover Mum's hair with a *hijab* or at least a white scarf. "We can easily do it using Photo Shop," said the graphic designer who worked on the poster.

Dad was adamant: "No ... Haya's poster must look like her: a beautiful woman, with subtle make-up and lovely wavy hair."

I and my two old comrades, Majdi and Ramzi, stayed late through the night talking and plotting, but this time with Omar.

"Me", I volunteered.

"No, you can't, you've got three little girls," objected Omar. Then added, "It's got to be me ... my life's over after Mum."

"How many Israelis are worth or equivalent to your Mum?" Ramzi's question was interrupted as Dad opened the door and stepped into the veranda.

"Listen, children, don't be foolish. I know exactly what you're plotting. Haya is dead and there's nothing you or I can do which will bring her back. She lived her life for you and for your children." Dad looked at me and continued: "If they are savages, we don't need to be like them. If you want to keep her memory alive and honour her, carry on with what she did for the needy and the poor. That's how you preserve her memory. I need you *all* to make me this promise right now."

He looked me in the eye and said: "Promise?"

Tears brimming, I said: "Promise."

It was Omar's turn.

"Omar, you've got to promise me." There was no reply. "I say, promise," Dad repeated.

At that point Omar stood up, kept quiet for a few seconds, then completely lost his temper: "Fuckers, criminals, they killed my mother and *you* want me to promise … and …" Omar's rage made his words completely incomprehensible.

Dad paid no attention to his anger and repeated: "Omar, I want you to promise me right now not to do anything stupid. Promise?"

"Okay, Dad, I promise." Omar walked away as tears flowed down his face.

Three days of mourning passed before I went into Mum's study. On her desk were her university books, exams and reports. Mum had gone back to university for a master's degree in Arabic literature. I couldn't help but smile when I saw her writing on *yet* another one of Dad's patients' notebooks. Remembered fondly her TC-WW records of the Seventies. I picked this one up and flipped through its many pages: it had long lists and hundreds of names: of the needy, the sick, the widowed, the injured, the unemployed, martyrs' families, houses demolished, prisoners, etc … the categories and the lists were extremely long. Much longer than her women's reception's (*istiqbal*) notebook.

I put her notebooks under my arm and kissed Dad and Omar a temporary goodbye.

I went to Jerusalem to see my three daughters, Zena, Maha and Zaha.

Soon after, both Omar and Dad turned religious.

10
Fadia

It was my father's love of a drink and my mother's love of chic attire that was a source of embarrassment in my childhood and youth, and a source of pride at a later age.

The high walls surrounding our villa in the town of Nablus separated the two contradictory worlds in which I comfortably lived, but often had to mediate.

Jordan's Nine Eleven
November 9, 2005
8:45 in the evening

White-on-White

Some were stunned, others were in total shock.

It was dark and dusty. You couldn't see a thing inside. Loads of people were rushing out in horror. Others, like Alma, were screaming in panic at a barricade of security men preventing them from reaching the hotel's lobby.

Out of the smoke appeared Hani. Before she could get to

her cousin, she glimpsed Ali's body being swung and dumped on the pavement outside. She threw herself on the ground next to Ali, started talking to him. She shook him. Hugged him. Kissed him. Then stood up, seeking help. Ambulances had finally begun to arrive. She made her way to one of the dazed nurses, and like many others, screamed at him for help. She grabbed him and dragged him forcibly by his uniform. He looked sideways towards where she was pointing, towards Ali. Screaming with pain she ultimately forced the frenzied nurses to pick Ali up and rush him into one of the many ambulances standing by. As she jumped into the ambulance with Ali, she realised she had stepped over various body parts and the flesh of another casualty sharing the ambulance with her beloved fiancé.

———————

White-on-White said the invitation card for tonight's party which was to precede the wedding, two days later, at the Intercontinental Hotel in the Red Sea town of al-'Aqabeh. All the women were instructed to wear white. The only colours permitted were on jewellery, and of make-up.

It was already winter in Montréal. For months now, summer clothing had disappeared from fancy shop windows. I first gave the shops a try, but soon opted for a fashion designer and his outrageous fees.

Alma, the bride, was my adored favourite niece.

I gladly joined Alma and her mother (my sister) on a dream-like shopping spree on the chic streets of Paris. There was nothing on earth we did not buy that week. All it took to have other fashionable boutiques rush to serve us like three spoiled princesses, was to pointedly carry a shopping bag from one expensive signé boutique in with us.

Alma's flashing beauty—and mine, of course—also helped.

We made our rounds between the elegant rue de Rivoli to the Avenue Montaigne; from rue de Faubourg Saint-Honoré to Avenue des Champs-Elysees; and from the trendy rue Bonaparte to Place de la Madeleine. The shopping lists included handbags from Gucci and vanity bags from Fendi, Chaumet jewellery, a selection from Creed Perfume Shop, morning dresses from Yves Saint Laurent, Christian Dior, Chanel and Pierre Cardin, and formal evening dresses from Pierre Balmain. They also included some presents for the groom; a few Charvet shirts and a pair or two of Berluti shoes.

It was during that *fairytale* bride's shopping spree in Paris that I finally understood why, some twenty-seven years ago, my mother, father and other members of my family had boycotted me and shunned me for more than five years.

I happily went along with the then fashionable, leftist, anti-establishment, anti-traditional, no-marriage ceremonies of the Seventies. My marriage to a left-leaning modest Christian excluded any pre-wedding shopping, no wedding ceremony, and of course no *white-on-white*, or for that matter, any *red-on-red* parties, either.

What I then believed was politically correct modesty, was conceived of as disgrace by my family.

Politically correct or disgraceful, my first marriage broke down in five years.

Unannounced, I decided to break my family's boycott.

Unannounced, I showed up at their doorstep.

My father was in total shock when I unexpectedly stepped

into his bedroom which was also his office. Not believing his own eyes, he began crying the minute he saw me next to his bed.

"What has happened to you? Why on earth do you look so dark and glum?" he said half-jokingly, trying to end the awkwardness of my five-year absence and the discomfort of our unanticipated encounter.

"I've been swimming lately, that's all."

"Did you have to sit in the sun for so long?"

I had to remind myself that whatever my father were to say that day, he was bound to be ill at ease. Of course, like most Arabs, he didn't like dark complexions. My white shirt and pants contrasted sharply with my dark suntan. I was wiping my tears as I walked towards my father who had been bed-ridden for the last twenty years. I hugged him tightly and together, we sobbed.

Soon after I was climbing the two flights of stairs that took me to the second floor living room where my mother and sister stood, speechless.

My mother's tight hugs and flowing tears brought me back into the family fold of emotions and warmth in no time. My sister's hesitation in greeting me reminded me of the never-changing family dynamics.

It must have been a sheer accident that I wore *white-on-white* the day I returned home, some twenty-two years ago.

It was on the evening of November 9th (the Jordanian nine-eleven, 2005) that *white-on-white* invitees, relatives and friends had arrived from all corners of the globe—Montréal, London, Paris, Athens, Beirut, New York, Dubai, Nablus, Ramallah, you name it—for the wedding.

145

My sister Huda was helping me zip up my tight white dress when the phone rang:

"Hi, Aunty Fadia, this is Alma. Can I come over just for a few minutes? I need to talk to you urgently before tonight's party."

"Hurry up, Alma, there's just a little time left. My brother Rais will be very unhappy if I arrive late."

"I promise I'll be there in no time!"

Alma looked absolutely beautiful in her Yves Saint Laurent white dress that evening.

Ageing is just terrible. I kept the thought to myself.

I got into the front seat next to Alma and she talked non-stop as we rode to my brother's house:

"Ple-e-e-ase, aunty, could you tell Mum not to keep inviting more of *her* friends to our wedding party, it's *our* wedding after all, not hers. She has got to understand this."

"Don't worry, love, I'll sort it all out with her tonight. Just drive safely and try not to be too late for Ali. He'll be waiting for you at the entrance of the Hyatt Regency."

I kissed Alma goodbye and walked into the courtyard entrance of my brother's villa. I entered through the slightly open door into the foyer. Rais was waiting there, looking extremely majestic for this grand occasion. There is something about Rais that gives me, and others around him, a strong feeling of reassurance. His physique; small piercing eyes, wavy black hair all contribute to this feeling. He was the oldest of six brothers and five sisters. As is often the case, Rais was patiently striding while waiting for other members of his family, all frantically rushing around the house trying to get ready for tonight's party.

I was admiring the gorgeous white dress, contrasting

beautifully with the dark hair and olive complexion of my petite and dainty sister-in-law, Maya, as she slowly descended the lobby's winding stairs. My nephew, Muneer, elegant in his black suit, was helping his mother from stepping on her dress's gown which trailed behind her.

Maya's dazzling looks made me sympathise more than ever with Alma's concern—it seemed that all the women in her family, not just her mother, were behaving as if both the pre-wedding party as well as the wedding itself were theirs, not Alma's and Ali's.

I could understand why *I*, having missed out on my own lavish wedding (let alone pre-wedding parties) would dress to kill tonight, but why should my sisters and sisters-in-law do that when they have *all* had their share of ceremonial extravagance?

See how out of style you become when you live almost all your life in occupied Palestine—perhaps that explains why, some six years ago, my second husband and I decided to migrate to Canada with our two teenage daughters and son.

I could see my brother looking impatiently at the five of us. His wife, Maya, me, his two endearing teenage daughters, Leila and Yara, and to a lesser extent his son Muneer, were standing, exchanging admiring remarks. Being a prominent political figure in Jordan, Rais often mediated between the two conflicting worlds in which he lived—the extravagance of his private family life, and the austerity of his public life in a country like Jordan.

Maya almost tripped on her gown when she rushed across the lobby to pick up the phone placed on top of a shining black breakfront.

"Hi, Jamileh . . ." I heard her say, before she went silent and then in no time, completely pale.

Though standing just a few meters away from Maya, we could all hear her close friend Jamileh screaming. Maya's distant eyes, her expressionless face, as well as the immediate tension in her body alerted us that something terrible had happened.

"Okay, okay, Jamileh, *habibti*, I will tell Rais and we will come right away. Just tell me where you are right now. Which hospital?"

"Oh, no, it sounds like Mustafa has had a heart attack," I hear Rais say, sighing.

Mustafa al-'Aqqad, a prominent Syrian film director and his wife, Jamileh, had just arrived from New York the day before, especially for the wedding.

As Rais asked Maya to hand him the receiver his own mobile rang.

"Hello . . . yes . . . yes . . . God . . . . Oh no! Radisson SAS . . . Sheraton . . . Oh, my God . . . did you say also in the Hyatt Regency? But that's where all our guests are . . . in the lobby waiting to be picked up . . . Oh, *GOD (la hawla wala quatta illa billah)*"

We were all totally stunned, desperately trying to figure out what was going on. By then, every single phone or mobile we had was ringing.

"For God's sake, where the hell is Alma? Is she with Ali?"

"Ask him about Hani, Rania, Uncle Sabih, Lama, 'Abeer . . ."
The list of names was getting longer and longer.

"How badly is he injured?"

"They have closed all the roads. The Shmesani and Jabal

148

Amman are totally blocked … how are we to reach the hospital?"

"Are they in two different hospitals?"

"Alma is okay, she says Ali is badly injured."

"Alma says she is in the hospital with Ali."

In the middle of huge chaos and total panic I heard Rais's commanding voice say:

"Okay, Maya, just take the car and try to get to Jamileh and Mustafa at al-Djani Hospital, he and Ali have been badly injured in an explosion in the lobby of the Hyatt Regency." Rais looked at his son and said: "Muneer, why don't you accompany your mother."

"Come on, Fadia, let's see to the rest. We need to get to poor Alma at Amman Hospital—apparently that's where Ali has been taken."

Perplexed, I ran behind Rais and got into the back seat next to him. Walid, the driver, was instructed to put on his emergency flashlights and proceed to Amman Hospital.

"Poor Alma, poor Ali." These were the only words I was capable of repeating as we drove short distances before being stopped by the numerous security checkpoints along the roads. The whole city looked like a madhouse; cars beeping, others going against the traffic, most diverted. A few like us were allowed to proceed to our destination because many security men recognised Rais.

Finally, we got to the emergency room at Amman Hospital.

Oh, God, what a scene. Realising the difficulty of the situation and my physiological state, Rais instructed me to wait outside as he proceeded into the room.

149

It was not long before Ali's two brothers arrived on the scene.

Speechless, we hugged and cried. By then everyone had realised how heartbreaking it all was.

Soon Alma emerged from the emergency area, clutching onto her Uncle Rais.

Everything about the way she looked told me that Ali had died.

There was no need for me to ask, and no need for her to tell.

Words were superfluous.

Before we knew it, Alma and I were clinging to one another—for the next few hours, and for days to come.

With an excruciating sense of emptiness Alma, Ali's two brothers and I drove away from the hospital.

We were on our way to Ali's mother.

Having failed to convince the many security barriers about her urgent need to get to her injured son, Ali's mother was aimlessly walking the streets of Amman. She had abandoned her car and later the many taxis she took, in despair. She was ultimately persuaded by her pleading daughter to just give up and return home. She did finally.

"Son ... they're all here except you."

Part Three

Expression, Memory and Power

As stomachs filled up, heads became tipsy and noise levels increased, more captivating topics seemed to be going round the table. Over-excited, I was trying to follow them all at the same time partly because, when I'm in a group, I often feel I'm missing a more interesting, more exciting or more important conversation than the one I'm having with the person next to me. And partly because the idea of writing this book was starting to ferment in my head. Being self-conscious spoilt the dinner for me: there is nothing worse than seeing one's friends and family members as 'potential characters' in a book.

But they were.

At one end, across the table from me, were Rana, Fadia and Reem. I could hear (but not necessarily follow) Fadia and Rana who were totally preoccupied with their wrinkles. Reem concentrated, while Rana and Fadia described the different techniques of facial plastic surgery at length; facelifts, botox and hydra fillings. I was amused by their animated chatter.

Fadia's palms were placed on either side of her face. Four of her fingers were stretching her facial muscles and skin towards her ears, while her two thumbs pulled her lower chin. Expressionless, Fadia was beginning to look like the eighty-year (eighty facelifts)-old Lebanese singer, Sabbouha.

Rana, who was sitting next to Fadia, was pulling her eyebrows to one side, thus making her frown lines disappear. Her forehead now, with this big distance between her stretched-out eyes, was looking like a cute little Chinese puppy's.

Meanwhile wrinkled Reem was giving it a shot by blowing out her cheeks, trying hard to get rid of the marionette lines at the corner of her mouth and the smile lines around her nose. If there is something beautiful about Reem, it is her smile and her smile lines.

Seeing my face, you could easily tell that I knew nothing about facial uplift. Like other CRIME members, I belonged to that generation in which wearing make-up or elegant clothing was considered anti-revolutionary. We were brought up to concentrate on our *minds* rather than our *bodies*.

Looking back, I no longer remember how the 'sexual revolution' of the Sixties and early Seventies succeeded when everybody was supposed to look asexual.

I guess looking asexual was sexy then.

With the mind getting fuzzy now, one realises the importance of looking sexy.

"How does it feel to be menopausal? How did you know you were there?" I overheard Maya asking veteran Aida. Pleased to be recognised as *the* menopause expert, Aida replied, emphasising every single word:

"The best part about menopause is that *there is no more*

sex—what a relief! It is complete freedom; it just feels great not to care about men any more. You don't have to look nice, you don't have to diet. Eat as much as you want and smoke as much as you want. You don't have to look elegant, so you dress comfortably. But most important: you realise how wonderful your women friends are. Look around this table. You can't imagine how much I love my menopause group: *I love them all.* They're my support and my true asset in life. They're what keep me in this weird place." As always, Aida was being melodramatic and Maya was praying for her menopause right then and there.

"Discreetly, we looked for a good plastic surgeon both in Amman and Beirut. We found out that botox fillings were better, safer and cheaper in Beirut, so we flew there. We wanted to surprise our husbands by looking younger, but they surprised us even more by not noticing . . ." As always Fadia managed to erupt into loud laughter.

What intrigued me much more than the botox details, was how easily they '*flew there*'. How on earth did they get visas for Beirut . . . when it is impossible for Palestinian passport holders to get a visa to most Arab countries, especially Syria and Lebanon?

I was thinking how, once again, it was the city of Beirut that united younger and older CRIME members; once the centre of brainstorming and revolutions, Beirut is now the centre for beauty makeovers.

That's globalisation.

My attention drifted to the other end of the table where hot political flashes were taking place between Ola (vehemently against Fatah), and Jamileh, a Fatah veteran (also against Fatah). I, like many others, sympathise easily with leftist, secularist Ola's anti-Fatah sentiments, but no one seemed to be able to understand the silver lining in Ola's almost pro-Hamas position: "*Today's vote was a protest vote against Fatah,*" she declared. "It may be true that Fatah has made fatal mistakes, but do you know what it means to have a protest vote? You're indirectly giving your vote to Hamas. Is that what you really want? You're only punishing yourself and a whole society by a protest vote." Jamileh's hot flashes were obvious: she was sweating, her cheeks were apple red, so were her eyes

"We either believe in democracy or we don't . . . If people want Hamas, then give them a chance to rule . . . we need to ask ourselves why Hamas has won people's hearts. You have no idea how much they resent Fatah and the Palestinian Authority. They've totally alienated everyone with their incompetence, corruption and lack of security . . ."

Realising that Ola could go on for ever, Jamileh interrupted her:

"I hope you don't think Hamas will save us! It will only take us back to 1973 PLO discussions: one state or two states; armed struggle or no armed struggle; violence or no violence; recognising Israel or not recognising Israel, and all the rest. Come on, we've seen it all. Once is enough. We don't need Hamas to repeat history, to lose another thirty years and find ourselves where we are today."

Jamileh's Moroccan accent was distinctly audible. Once Jamileh and Ola started arguing in their own accents, Moroccan and Egyptian, I knew it was getting serious.

Varda, another menopause expert, was getting tired of Ola's

and Jamileh's political arguments—she had heard the Fatah-Hamas debate too many times lately.

She turned her back on them and joined Maya's and Aida's menopause: "Believe me, darling, you know it when you get there. I think psychologists should add 'monstrous fifties' to their 'terrible twos and fours'."

"What was that? I didn't understand, repeat please," said Maya.

"You know, in child psychology, we have what we call the terrible twos and the terrible fours—all that children can say at the age of two is, 'NO . . . NO,' and all that they can say at the age of four is, 'NO . . . NO . . . don't want to share . . . this is *mine*.' So I think psychologists should also add 'monstrous fifties' to their list."

"I was afraid to go to Beirut all by myself so I tricked Sawsan, my sister in-law, and Maya into coming along. For two weeks I made nasty remarks about their wrinkles till one day they fell into the trap," continued Fadia.

"But what have Fatah done about the Occupation? What have they done about boycotting Israeli products? What have they done for women? Where are the institutions that Arafat built? Did they all collapse with his death?"

"Hamas is only getting stronger because Arafat and his authority were undermined by Israel, by Sharon specifically. And, of course, the Americans and the Europeans followed. By undermining Arafat and Fatah you're only empowering Hamas and fundamentalism, who else? Look at the leftist parties!"

"For God's sake, give them a chance! Fatah ruled for forty-some years, it's time for a change, believe me, change is good for all."

Only now did I take note that the PLO had been in power for the last forty-two years (1964–2006). No wonder it is showing serious menopausal symptoms like us.

Arafat could easily have done with one or two plastic surgeries on his face.

Who knows, maybe he went through a bad lip augmentation.

"At least Fatah is a secular movement—what horrifies me is Hamas' social agenda, not their political programme (since Israel won't budge either for Fatah or for Hamas). It is we women who will end up paying a heavy price."

"You must be kidding! What have Fatah, or for that matter the five leftist parties, done by being secular movements? What have they done for women? What? One or two ministers and seven out of a hundred and thirty-two parliament members! Come on, you have to understand that since the Oslo Peace Accord, Hamas has become the *only* grassroots organisation. It has become popular because of its social programmes, its kindergartens, its schools, its medical services. And meanwhile the Palestinian Authority has encouraged corruption."

Not wanting to interfere in the internal affairs of Palestine, Ruth joined the menopausal discussion: "You know you're menopausal when all your 'maybe(s)' and 'perhaps' are replaced by 'I am dead certain.'"

At that point I wanted to ask Ruth if this meant that Israel had been menopausal all along, but it was too noisy for her to hear me.

"Finally, they were after me to make an appointment with the Lebanese plastic surgeon. The three of us crossed the bridge to Amman and next day we flew into Beirut airport and went directly to the American University hospital."

"If the leftist parties had even a bit of respect for their constituencies, they would have united. Look at them, they formed five different groups and why? Because each one wanted to be the head of the list, so each made his or her own list!"

"I almost fainted when I saw the surgeon filling the huge botox needle. He had marked all my wrinkles on his computer: two sides of my mouth, the lower part of my cheeks, my upper lip, down the chin, up the neck and, in Maya's case, the deep line between her eyebrows."

"At first you think it's funny, then you realise the seriousness of the situation. You go to see your gynaecologist and in a matter of fact tone he says: 'Ya . . . you're at that *critical age*, don't worry, it will pass.' But the problem arises when it doesn't and you start having all sorts of physical problems: high blood pressure, heart palpitations, stomach aches, you become anxious, bitter, angry, and all the rest."

"Pointless, the wrinkles were back in less than two months . . . three at most. Not only that, poor Sawsan, one of her botox fillings shifted and formed a ball right next to her nose. They had to operate and take it out. She swore she would never do it again."

"The problem is American and European unconditional love for Israel. Israel keeps destroying European-funded projects in Palestine, and instead of forcing Israel to pay for them the Europeans fork out once again."

Across the table from me sat Luisa, her chit-chat oscillating between love stories and today's election stories:

"It was September of 1991, the last time I ever truly fell in love. And what happened? I got a phone call from Zahira Kamal (a PLO functionary) inviting me to come to Madrid to attend the Grand Opening of the Middle East International Peace Conference. I had to choose between my new love and Palestine—and you all know what I chose."

Even though this was meant as a joke, it made my cry.

I started thinking how many women around this table had left behind dear ones for Palestine. It reminded me of the one line I loved most in *Bab il-Saha*, Sahar Khalifeh's book, *Port of the Square*: 'Palestine is a beast who devours her children.'

Exhausted Jamileh soon defected to the menopause talk: "Listen, it's very simple, you know you are menopausal when *all* your days become as bad as the day before your monthly period. You also know it when that BAD person, who is responsible for it all, appears and you're about to strangle him, or her, of course. That is how you know you are menopausal."

Rana's high-pitched voice caught my ear.

"Botox is passé, I highly recommend the Brazilian technique but it should *only* be done in Brazil—we can combine Carnival with a facelift." After loud laughter she continued: "What they do there is paralyse some facial nerves, especially those in the forehead, this way you lose the nerve and all your wrinkles disappear."

"You mean all facial expressions disappear?" I asked, terrified.

"Yes . . . What do we need facial expressions for these days?" replied Rana.

Luisa was bragging about how transparent and democratic the elections had been today. Terrified that Hamas might win a substantial percentage, I wanted to tell Luisa that they (meaning the European Union) and we Palestinians could probably have done with a bit less transparency and democracy for now!

Flora, a self-hating PLO and good poker player, who hardly ever reveals her private life, spoke up coolly: "I think menopause is a middle class professional women's phenomenon. Look at women in villages and refugee camps. They accept their age, they accept their wrinkles, they accept that there is no more sex in their lives, they accept that they are losing authority and power, and hence act accordingly. Unlike us, at fifty plus, we want to look thirty-five, that's why we are anxious, angry and frustrated. We refuse to accept new realities, we want to have eternal youth and power. It doesn't work."

It was no longer clear to me whether Flora was referring to botox, Hamas, or menopause. As the long night dwindled, CRIME members got exhausted and all issues, arguments, clashes and flashes began merging: all were anxious, all seemed to be in total denial, and all were having difficulty accepting new realities: whether they were wrinkles, ageing or Hamas.

All seemed to be having difficulties with expression, memory and power.

The day after, Hamas had a sweeping victory.

Experts say: Menopause is a wake-up call for a new phase in your life.

And I say: So is Hamas.

Two wake-up calls may be more than most people can handle.